KOREA

Democracy on Trial

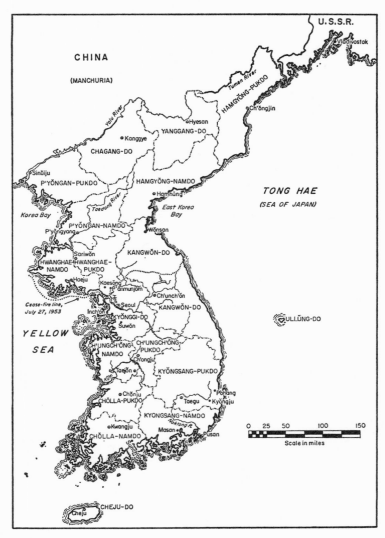

CHINA

(MANCHURIA)

U.S.S.R.

Vladivostok

Yalu River

Tuman River

HAMGYŎNG-PUKDO

Ch'ŏngjin

Hyesan

YANGGANG-DO

Kanggye

CHAGANG-DO

Sinŭiju

P'YŎNGAN-PUKDO

HAMGYŎNG-NAMDO

Hamhŭng

Taedong River

East Korea
Bay

TONG HAE

(SEA OF JAPAN)

Korea Bay

P'YŎNGAN-NAMDO

P'yŏngyang

Wŏnsan

Sariwŏn

KANGWŎN-DO

HWANGHAE- HWANGHAE-
NAMDO   PUKDO

Haeju

Kaesŏng

P'anmunjŏm

Ch'unch'ŏn

Cease-fire line,
July 27, 1953

Inch'ŏn

Seoul

KANGWŎN-DO

KYŎNGGI-DO

Suwŏn

ULLŬNG-DO

YELLOW

SEA

CH'UNGCH'ŎNG-
NAMDO

CH'UNGCH'ŎNG-
PUKDO

Ch'ŏngju

Taejŏn

KYŎNGSANG-PUKDO

Chŏnju

CHŎLLA-PUKDO

Taegu

Pohang

Kyŏngju

KYŎNGSANG-NAMDO

Naktong R.

Kwangju

CHŎLLA-NAMDO

Masan

Pusan

0   25   50   100   150

Scale in miles

Cheju

CHEJU-DO

KOREA

KOREA

Democracy on Trial

JOHN KIE-CHIANG OH
Marquette University

CORNELL UNIVERSITY PRESS
Ithaca and London

First published 1968
Second printing 1970

International Standard Book Number 0-8014-0322-7

Library of Congress Catalog Card Number 68-26693

PRINTED IN THE UNITED STATES OF AMERICA
BY VALLEY OFFSET, INC.

TO MY WIFE AND
OUR CHILDREN

Preface

Shortly after the Second World War, democracy was hailed as the ideal guiding principle for emerging nations of the non-Communist world. Since then, however, democracy has been subject to the crushing burdens of political realities in each state that adopted it. It has clashed head on with authoritarian ideologies and practices, both old and new. In a world divided, still partly on the basis of ideology, the ideological orientation of the newly independent states toward, or away from, democracy is a significant question.

Probably nowhere in the world has this problem been brought into sharper focus than in Korea, which was divided into the American and Soviet zones in 1945. As in other divided nations, the intense and multifarious competition that ensued between the southern and northern halves of the Korean peninsula could be generalized, among other ways, as a contest between the systems of democracy and communism.

Briefly, this work is a study of how Western democracy fared in the political and governmental development of a re-emerging East Asian nation, South Korea. In the little over two decades since the end of the Second World War, South Korea has experienced a series of political upheavals. She was liberated from the Japanese colonial domination in

1945 to be placed under the United States military government for three years. The Republic of Korea, with a "democratic" constitution and numerous other features of a representative government, was established in 1948 under American-educated President Syngman Rhee (Yi Sŭng-man). His regime, however, was violently overthrown by the Student Uprising in 1960. Subsequently, the Second Republic under Premier John M. Chang (Chang Myŏn) was jubilantly inaugurated, only to be toppled nine months later by a few thousand soldiers personally commanded by then Major General Chung Hee Park (Pak Chŏng-hi), the General-turned-President of the Third Republic since December, 1963. In May, 1967, President Park was re-elected to his second—and constitutionally last—term of office.

It is noteworthy that the United States has been directly and continuously involved in Korean affairs since 1945. That the United States suffered 157,530 casualties, including 33,629 battle deaths, during the three years of the Korean War was a most concrete evidence of this involvement, which continues today in South Korea, most obviously through the seemingly perennial presence of American troops in the divided peninsula.

As in the case of most other emerging nations, South Korea has faced numerous political problems. They have included the legacies of a harsh colonial rule for over a generation, the unnatural division of the country into a Communist-dominated portion and the Western-aligned part, the resurgence of the old and peculiarly indigenous political patterns, the influx of foreign ideologies, the importation of alien systems, the extensive involvement of not only the United States but also the United Nations in the state-building process, a full-scale invasion of the infant republic by the Communist armed forces, the bloody war that ravaged the depth and width of the peninsula, the "revolution of rising expectations," a violent popular uprising that actually toppled a seemingly impregnable regime, the tumult of a military coup, the rule by decrees of a military junta, and the entrenchment of the Third Republic.

This study analyzes these problems to the extent they are relevant to the central theme—democracy on trial. Part I discusses the period from August, 1948, to May, 1961. It was during this turbulent period that the Korean people, having regained independence, had to cope with the problems of the establishment and drastic alteration of a democratic superstructure in South Korea. The Student Uprising also took place in this thirteen-year period of the brightest hope and the darkest despair. Part II discusses the more recent developments since the May, 1961, *coup d'état*, a significant turning point in an analysis of democracy on trial, and examines the considerable transformation of political patterns, governmental systems, and processes since the coup. It analyzes, therefore, what appears to be a fundamental modification of the basic political orientation of Korea that occurred with the inglorious demise of the "democratic" Second Republic. Although Korea had been hoped to become a "beacon light of democracy in the Far East," she has apparently joined the ranks of many emergent nations in which the political role of the military has become decisive.

A definition of democracy might be delineated here as follows: it is a philosophy of socio-political organization and functions in which major public policies are decided on the majority principle and executed by public officials subject to popular control at periodic elections, conducted on the principle of political equality and under conditions of political freedom. One cannot, without qualifications, equate democracy as defined here with that of the Western world. Nevertheless, the more notable Western nations have developed political traditions, principles, assumptions, and systems out of which the term "democracy" has acquired concrete meanings. Britain, Canada, and the United States, for instance, may be named as the prime examples of such nations. The term "Western democracy" is used, therefore, when necessary to distinguish it from other versions of democracy preceded by adjectives such as "people's" or "guided."

This work is based on materials in Korean, English, and some Japanese. I have examined relevant sources in South Korea, at the Library of Congress, the East Asian Library of Columbia University, the Harvard-Yenching Institute Library, and the University of Chicago Library. I secured some data for this work during my visit to Korea in 1961 and subsequently had some pertinent materials shipped to me from that country. The Postscript is the result of my trip to Korea in the summer of 1967. I have made every attempt to interview as many key persons involved in Korean development as possible, although such opportunities have been limited.

In general, the transliteration of Korean names and terms in this study conforms to the McCune-Reischauer system, with a few common exceptions such as Syngman Rhee, Chung Hee Park, and Seoul. As a general rule, the family name is presented first, and the first and middle names are connected with a hyphen.

I wish to disavow any interest whatever in making a case for or against any individuals or groups. If any part of this study offends the particular sensitivities, convictions, or loyalties of any individuals or groups, I can only apologize to them and ask for their understanding that I have aimed at objectivity to the best of my ability.

JOHN KIE-CHIANG OH

Milwaukee, Wisconsin
February 1968

Acknowledgments

I owe my profound gratitude to many individuals and institutions whose unwavering confidence in me has made this study possible. I would like to acknowledge my particular indebtedness to the Louis W. and Maud Hill Family Foundation, St. Paul, Minnesota, which extended a research grant to me for the summer of 1964, and also to the Elizabeth C. Quinlan Foundation, Minneapolis, Minnesota, for its research support for the summer of 1965. Without their generous grants, this study would have been impossible. I would like to express my sincere appreciation to Msgr. Terrence J. Murphy, president of the College of St. Thomas, St. Paul, Minnesota, who personally introduced me to these foundations and unreservedly recommended my project for their support.

My appreciation is also expressed to the distinguished members of the Marquette University Committee on Research, who cast their votes of confidence in me and provided generous support for my trip to Korea and Japan during the summer of 1967, which enabled me to add the Postscript to this work and to begin my research project on contemporary Japan.

I benefited greatly from informal conversations with scholars, political leaders, and diplomatic and military personnel, who are too numerous to be named here. I would like to thank my father for shipping newspapers and periodicals from Korea to me so regularly and for so many years.

Many thanks are due to Mr. Key P. Yang of the Orientalia Division and Dr. Cho Sŏng-yun of the Law Library, both of the Library of Congress. I also appreciated the cooperation of Mr. Kim Sŏng-ha of the Harvard-Yenching Institute Library during my sojourn in Cambridge in the summer of 1965. I would like to thank the staff of Cornell University Press, who processed my manuscript carefully and competently. I would also like to thank my graduate assistants at Marquette University—Martha M. Wynn, Patricia Ann O'Connor, and Joseph P. Heim—for their always cheerful cooperation.

Finally, I owe a heartfelt thanks which I have rarely expressed to my wife, Bongwan (Bonnie) Cho. She volunteered to type the original, much longer version of this book even while busily engaged in her doctoral studies and in running a home. Without her implicit understanding, I would not have been able to continue the prolonged labor of completing this study, a task that too often diverted my time from being spent with her and our three darling children.

Contents

Map

Tables

PART I

DEMOCRACY IN THE KOREAN REPUBLIC

Chapter 1

Launching the Republic

In the Cairo Declaration of December 1, 1943, the United States, Britain, and China agreed that "in due course" Korea should become free and independent.[1] Subsequently, at the end of World War II, Korea was freed from Japanese colonial domination only to be placed under American and Soviet occupation. The armies of occupation quickly divided the peninsula, which had remained united even during the thirty-five years of Japanese rule. The United States Armed Forces in Korea (USAFIK) was established on September 8, 1945, to begin the difficult and thankless task of ruling a "liberated people" impatient for immediate and complete independence.

The erosion of the wartime alliance between the United States and the Soviet Union made it increasingly difficult for the two powers to agree on the political future of Korea.[2] With each failure in American-Soviet negotiations, their positions on divided Korea hardened perceptibly. After the first American-Soviet joint commission, which met in Seoul, adjourned on May 8, 1946, hope faded for an early abolition of the dividing line at the 38th parallel. The impasse marked a turning point in the activities of the two occupying powers.

The Soviet occupation government intensified its policy of

communizing North Korea. The North Korean Provisional People's Committee was established in P'yŏngyang as early as February, 1946, "as a precursor of a regime to be inaugurated later," [3] and the North Korean Workers' Party, which united the dominant Communist groups, was launched in July of that year. The American authorities turned their attention to the suppression of Communist agitators in the south and to gradual relinquishment of some administrative responsibilities to Koreans. The 38th parallel, which had initially been intended as a military expedience between two allies, became a formidable wall separating two opposing powers and their local clienteles, an effective barrier between Communist North Korea and the American-influenced south. Hence, North Korea is not of immediate concern for this study, except in cases where activities in the north impinged on the problems and issues of South Korea.

The Tortuous Path

In the spring of 1947, after nearly two years of apparent indecision as to what the official American attitude toward Communist expansion should be, the United States launched its "containment" policy, explicated by President Truman on March 12, 1947, in his offer of aid to Greece and Turkey. The repercussions of this development in American policy were felt in most of the problem areas of the world, including Korea. The Joint Commission, which had vainly attempted to establish a "democratic government for a unified Korea," now lost its *raison d'être*, as it again reached a deadlock in June, 1947.

"In view of the inability of the Joint Commission to reach agreement," [4] the United States decided to take the Korean question to the United Nations. From the American point of view, the need to break the deadlock must have begun to seem urgent. Discussion of Korean policy had evidently taken place at the highest levels of American government. The armed services pressed for an early end to the occupation; Congress had slashed defense appropriations in the postwar period, and the occupation was expensive, in manpower as well as money. Perhaps it was also taking its toll on the nerves of those who had the task of defending a perilous strategic area.[5] The State Department was hesitant about ending the occupation, however, for fear that the whole of Korea might quickly fall to the highly organized Communists of the north and their followers in the southern zone.[6]

At the same moment that the Soviet Union was notified of this American decision to bring the Korean question to the United Nations, the United States delegation asked that "the Problem of the Independence of Korea" be placed on the agenda of the General Assembly.[7] From then on, the diplomatic activity involving Korean independence centered around the United Nations, and Korea apparently became a problem of this organization. The United States still remained the prime mover in disposing the problem.

Despite vocal Soviet opposition, the General Assembly on November 14, 1947, adopted a resolution calling for significant actions in Korea—by forty-three votes to six, with six abstentions. The resolution established a United Nations Temporary Commission on Korea (UNTCOK) and recommended:

that the elections be held not later than 31 March 1948 on the basis of adult suffrage and by secret ballot to choose representatives with whom the Commission may consult regarding the prompt attainment of the freedom and independence of the Korean people and which representatives, constituting a National Assembly, may establish a National Government of Korea. The number of representatives from each voting area or zone should be proportionate to the population, and the elections should be under the observation of the Commission.

The resolution further recommended that, immediately upon the establishment of a national government, the government should:

(*a*) constitute its own national security forces and dissolve all military or semi-military formations not included therein; (*b*) take over the functions of government from the military commands and civilian authorities of north and south Korea; and (*c*) arrange with the occupying Powers for the complete withdrawal from Korea of their armed forces as early as practicable and if possible within ninety days.[8]

Apparently the resolution envisioned that the new government would administer all of Korea and the problem of the division of the country would be liquidated. Since the people of Korea would hold an election to select representatives who would form a government, the problem of deciding who should speak for Korea in the United Nations would also be resolved. Obviously, the Temporary Commission's mandate was to accomplish what the United States and the Soviet Union had been unable to do through bilateral negotiations.[9]

The U.N. Temporary Commission held its first meeting in Seoul on January 12, 1948. Northern Korea was barred from it, however, because the Soviet occupation army flatly refused to cooperate with the commission. Unable to perform its functions in northern Korea, the commission had to consider whether or not it should proceed with carrying out the General Assembly's program in southern Korea alone.

Preliminary consultations with South Korean political leaders indicated a sharp division of opinion. Except for Kim Koo (Kim Ku) and his Korean Independence Party, the rightist groups appeared to be in favor of immediate elections, even if only for southern Korea: "Half a loaf is better than none." [10] Dr. Rhee, then chairman of the Association for the Rapid Realization of Korean Independence, not only thought elections should be held in South Korea, but believed that it would be possible "to complete an election within four weeks." [11] The leaders of moderate and leftist groups, however, were strongly opposed to holding elections in South Korea alone, arguing that the voting would delay and complicate the country's unification.

Some influential voices in the United States urged immediate elections. For instance, a *New York Times* editorial stated:

Hard as it is, the choice should be made to go ahead with elections and establishment of a government in South Korea. Then the twenty million people of that area—two-thirds of Korea's population—at least will have a fighting chance to maintain order and develop their country along democratic lines once occupation forces are withdrawn.[12]

The United States government decided that there was no choice and on February 26, 1948, effected the adoption of another United Nations resolution directing the Temporary Commission in Seoul to observe elections "in as much of Korea as is accessible to it." [13] In an appendix to this resolution, the Interim Committee established by the General Assembly stated its assumption that the election would be held only if a "free atmosphere" were found to exist; presumably this stipulation was to ensure a democratic process.

The first general elections in Korean history, to elect the members of the National Assembly, were scheduled for May 10—a little over two months after the decision of the Interim Committee.[14] The preparations for the general elections were

hardly carried out in an ideal atmosphere. The Communists
in both southern and northern Korea were vehemently opposed to the United Nations–sponsored elections. Communist-
inspired riots in February, 1948, caused at least thirty-seven
deaths and more than 8,000 arrests in southern Korea and
created an air of suspicion and unrest which the Temporary
Commission viewed with extreme concern.[15]

Kim Ku and Kim Kyu-sik then suddenly proposed a conference of political leaders in both southern and northern
Korea to discuss possible means of resolving the differences
between the two zones and unifying the country. Radio
P'yŏngyang announced that the North Korean People's Committee invited many of the political leaders in South Korea—
excluding Dr. Rhee—to attend a coalition conference in
P'yŏngyang to discuss the formation of a unified government.
This invitation immediately drew criticism from the American
command and most of the southern rightist elements, who denounced it as a Soviet attempt to seize countrywide power.[16]

Despite such opposition, more than fifty political leaders
in South Korea, including Kim Ku and Kim Kyu-sik, attended
the "coalition conference" in P'yŏngyang on April 22 and
23.[17] The conference passed a resolution calling for the formation of a unified Korean government, the rejection of dictatorship and "monopolistic capitalism," and the immediate
withdrawal of American and Soviet occupying troops, and
voiced opposition to the establishment of foreign military
bases on Korean soil. Whatever the motives of these southern
leaders who attended the P'yŏngyang conference, their efforts
at unity were to be abortive. Many South Koreans believed
them to be dupes in the propaganda offensive launched by
the North Korean Communists against the proposed elections.[18]

These developments crystallized the division within the

rightist and moderate elements in South Korea. For those who attended the conference and decided to boycott the proposed May 10 elections, the "separate" elections for a "separate" government could not be legitimate. Thus the elections were to establish a government whose legitimacy was to be denied not only by the Communists in North Korea but by some rightists and moderates in South Korea as well.

As the Communists predictably opened a drive to disrupt the elections by sabotage and terrorism, tension mounted dangerously in South Korea. Fire was used to fight fire. The rightists who participated actively in the elections went so far as to label almost all nonrightists and nonparticipants as Communists. Extremists in each political wing formed terrorist bands. To maintain law and order during the election period, the American military government authorized the police to deputize large bands of "loyal citizens," the Community Protective Associations. Their membership was necessarily drawn from among rightists and, in some instances, from terrorist youth organizations.

The figures later released by the South Korean Interim Government concerning the casualties that attended the elections suggested that the election period was far from tranquil and that improper pressure had been exerted by officials and terrorist groups. Between March 29 and May 19, 589 persons, classified as follows, were killed in South Korea: 63 policemen, 9 members of policemen's families, 37 government officials and candidates for election, 150 civilians (presumably members of the Protective Associations), and 330 "rioters." In addition, considerable property destruction and personal injury resulted from the at least 1,047 cases of "assaults and violences by the elements of the South Korean Labor Party."[19] On the election day itself, 44 persons were killed and 62 wounded throughout South Korea.

Amid all these bloody disturbances, 7,837,504 voters had registered by the end of the registration period, and 7,036,750 of them, or about 95.2 per cent of the total registrants, actually took part in the voting. According to the U.N. Temporary Commission, this figure represented 75 per cent of the total potential voters, who were estimated by the South Korean Interim Government at 9,834,000. The estimated total population on April 1, 1949, was 19,947,000.[20]

Dr. Rhee was quick to set the tone in evaluating the nature and outcome of the elections: "It was the solidarity of the people that made the election a complete success to the marvel of our friendly neighbors. The consequent national legislature is *truly democratic in character*." [21] The American military government and the South Korean Interim Government described the elections as a "great victory for democracy and repudiation of communism," although many unofficial reports were less favorable.[22]

The U.N. Temporary Commission reasoned:

The fact that 75 per cent of the potential voters actually went to the polls would be regarded in most countries as an impressive popular response. Even after making full allowance for the possible effect of social pressure on some of the voters and for the habits of subordination to authority in producing a large vote, this response still signified on the part of the people a widespread endorsement of the elections as a means of achieving Korean independence, and an acceptance of those parties and individuals that campaigned for the elections.[23]

On the basis of this reasoning, the commission resolved:

To record its opinion that the results of the ballots of 10 May 1948 are a valid expression of the free will of the electorate in those parts of Korea which were accessible to the Commission and in which the inhabitants constituted approximately two-thirds of the people of all Korea.[24]

The United States government, through John Foster Dulles, advised the First Committee of the General Assembly that the elections "constituted a magnificent demonstration of the capacity of the Korean people to establish a representative and responsible government." [25] On December 12, 1948, five days after the Dulles talk, the General Assembly adopted a resolution declaring:

There has been established a lawful government (the Government of the Republic of Korea) having effective control and jurisdiction over that part of Korea where the Temporary Commission was able to observe and consult and in which the great majority of the people of all Korea reside; that this Government is based on elections which were a valid expression of the free will of the electorate of that part of Korea and which were observed by the Temporary Commission; and that it is the only such Government in Korea. [26]

The resolution also decided that, in order to achieve the objectives set forth in the resolution of November 14, 1947, a "Commission on Korea," consisting of Australia, China, El Salvador, France, India, the Philippines, and Syria, should be established to continue the work of the Temporary Commission.

The General Assembly of the United Nations thus committed its prestige in support of the newly acquired "mandate" of the South Korean government as the only lawful government in Korea. The General Assembly obviously failed to take cognizance of problematical and undemocratic practices in the elections; instead, it committed itself to the view that the elections were "a valid expression of the free will" of the Korean people. Furthermore, the General Assembly, on the basis of these views, chose to remain involved in Korean affairs by appointing a U.N. commission on Korea—striking out the term "temporary" that had modified the title of its predecessor.

Although no party gained anything approaching a majority of the two hundred National Assembly seats in the elections, Rhee's Association for the Rapid Realization of Independence obtained fifty-five seats and the conservative Hanguk (Korean) Democratic Party, headed by Kim Sŏng-su, secured twenty-nine. Two right-wing "youth organizations," the Taedong Youth Corps, led by Yi Ch'ŏng-ch'ŏn, and the National Youth Corps, led by Yi Pŏm-sŏk, won twelve and six seats respectively. Representatives of minor parties and eighty-five independents—many of whom were declared rightists—rounded out the Assembly.[27] The conservative, rightist complexion of the new Assembly stemmed from several factors: the boycott by the leftists, the moderates, and Kim Ku's followers and the essential conservatism of Korea, as well as the obvious fact of Rhee's personal popularity.[28] No less than forty-eight "political parties and social organizations" were represented by one or more elected assemblymen. The number of various organizations that had run candidates but failed to elect any far exceeded forty-eight. Possibly because of the superabundance of organizations running candidates and the intense enmity among them, 42.5 per cent of the elected members declared themselves "independents." [29]

When the National Assembly convened for the first time on May 31, Rhee was elected as Assembly chairman—a first step to the presidency of the Republic. It is noteworthy that in the first vote for chairmanship of the National Assembly, Rhee won 188 votes out of a possible 198, and that the Hanguk Democratic Party did not nominate an opposing candidate. This almost unanimous accord for Rhee in the Assembly, however, was to be short-lived; Rhee's advocacy of a presi-

dential system in the new government was quite opposed to
the views of other Assembly members, particularly those from
the Hanguk Democratic Party, who favored a cabinet system.
The Hanguk Democrats were willing to elect Rhee as President of the Republic, with the expectation that they would
hold the helm of the administration under a cabinet system.[30]

Chairman Rhee now proceeded to make his appointments,
including the membership of the Constitution-Drafting Committee.[31] The Assembly was obliged to work rapidly, because
the American military government's timetable called for vest-
ing the new government with its powers on August 15, only
two and a half months after the initial meeting of the First
Korean National Assembly. The task of drafting a completely
new constitution on short notice was a difficult one for the Assembly, particularly in view of the fact that the backgrounds
of the elected assemblymen indicated little professional adapt-
ability or aptitude for tasks such as this (see Table 1). Never-

Table 1. Occupational backgrounds of the assemblymen, 1948

Occupation	Number
Farmers	84
Merchants	25
Journalists and publishers	16
Politicians	14
Medical doctors	10
Clergy	8
Authors and educators	8
Lawyers and judges	5
No declared occupation	20
Miscellaneous	8
Total	198

Source: Republic of Korea, House of Representatives, Taehan
minguk kukhoe kaekwan (Survey of the National Assembly of the
Republic of Korea) (Seoul: Minŭiwŏn samuch'ŏ, 1959).

theless, a constitution was adopted and promulgated by July 17, 1948—scarcely a month and a half after the establishment of the Assembly.

Governmental Framework

The political heritage of the Korean people up to 1948, when the Republic was hastily established, contained little to suggest the birth of a stable constitutionalism. Korea's traditional monarchical system was superseded in 1910 by a militaristic colonial domination that lasted until 1945. Three years of American military government followed. As a result, the Korean people had received little practical training for a modern or democratic constitutionalism.

Most South Koreans in 1948 were primarily interested in a life free from political oppression and economic deprivation—without having a clear notion of how these could be achieved. Certainly, they knew next to nothing about democratic constitutionalism. The adoption of a political system for the fledgling state was left up to the new, nationalistic political elite, which now included the newly elected assemblymen, the first generation of legislators in Korean history.

Leaders of the new state realized that the occasion of state-building was a golden opportunity to modernize the Korean polity. They also believed that they had to adopt a system that would be compatible with the wave of the future. The Korean intelligentsia were familiar with Western, democratic polities, and the victory of the "democratic" coalitions in two world wars appeared to them to indicate that democratic forms of government represented progress and enlightenment. At the same time, demonstrating that the new elite could establish democratic-constitutional forms of government would display Korea's cultural equality to the world powers. The thirty-odd framers of the Korean constitution were laboring in a period when the claim "to be democratic carried the presumption of respectability." [32] Even the former colonial master of Korea, neighboring Japan, already had as of May, 1947, a strikingly "democratic" constitution, largely drafted by the government section of General MacArthur's headquarters. Moreover, the members of the committee had a vague sense of "mandate" from the public at large to establish a representative framework.[33] In any case, after a month and a half of work, the framers presented to the National Assembly a "democratic" constitution for official adoption.

The constitution was adopted by the National Assembly on July 12 and promulgated five days later, on July 17, 1948. It was a lengthy document—although some constitutions, such as the Indian fundamental law, have been much longer—containing 10 chapters, 102 articles, and a rather long preamble. The preamble, in part, declared that the Koreans were engaged in the "re-establishment" of a "democratic" and independent state and were determined:

To establish a democratic system of government eliminating evil social customs of all kinds,

To afford equal opportunities to every person and to provide for the fullest development of the capacity of each individual in all the fields of political, economic, social and cultural life.[34]

The "General Provisions" in Chapter I declared that the Republic of Korea "shall be a democratic and republican state" and that "the sovereignty of the Republic of Korea shall reside in the people," from whom all state authority emanates. Article 5 stated that in all fields of political, economic, social, and cultural life, the Republic of Korea "shall be responsible for respecting and guaranteeing the liberty, equality and initiative of each individual and for protecting and adjusting these for the purpose of promoting the general welfare." The chapter also renounced all aggressive wars, placing upon the military the mission of performing "the sacred duty of protecting the country."

The rights and duties of citizens of the Republic were spelled out in Chapter II, which listed specifically those basic rights guaranteed in the first chapter. These included equality before the law, "personal liberty," freedom of domicile, freedom from trespass and unlawful search, freedom of private correspondence, "the freedom of speech, press, assembly and association," "the right of property," "equal opportunity of education," "the equality of men and women," and the rights to elect public officials and hold public office. Article 27 also stated that "public officials shall be the trustees of the sovereign people and shall at all times be responsible to the people." "Little fault could be found with the democratic nature of this chapter" [35]—thus far.

Article 28, however, qualified all the preceding articles by stipulating that "laws imposing restrictions upon the liberties and rights of citizens shall be enacted only when necessary for the maintenance of public order or the welfare of the community." The freedoms mentioned in preceding articles were guaranteed, but with such qualifications as "except as specified by law," "except in accordance with law," and "with the provisions of the law." Thus, when deemed "necessary" by ruling powers "for the maintenance of public order or the welfare of the community," all these liberties could be restricted "with the provision of the law." [36] In the hands of the ruling power, these qualifications were potential restrictions and weapons that could be applied against any of the freedoms so beautifully enumerated and "guaranteed" in the Constitution.

The fundamental law then turned to the establishment of

the framework of government. According to Chapter III, the National Assembly was to exercise the legislative power. It was provided that members of the two-house Assembly be chosen, for four-year terms in the House of Representatives and six years in the House of Councilors, "by universal, equal, direct, and secret vote." The National Assembly would convene once a year and could be called into "extraordinary" session by the President of the Republic or upon request of one-fourth of the legislators. No provision was made for dissolution of the National Assembly before the end of the House of Representatives' four-year term.

Bills could be introduced by members of the National Assembly or by the executive. Passage was by majority vote, and in case of a presidential veto, two-thirds of a quorum could override it, with two-thirds of the members of the Assembly constituting a quorum. The legislature concurred in the executive's administration of foreign affairs and considered and decided upon budgets. On the latter subject its actions were restricted to the budget given to it for consideration by the executive.

On paper, anyway, the legislature also had the power to institute impeachment proceedings against the President, the Vice-President, members of the State Council (cabinet), the Chairman of the Board of Audit, judges, and other public officials designated by law, when they "violated in the exercise of their duties, provisions of this Constitution or other laws."

The President of the Republic, elected for a four-year term by two-thirds of the National Assembly members, was the executive head of the government. He had the usual powers of representing the state in foreign relations, of signing and executing the laws, and of standing as the head of the military establishment.

As to the State Council, the Constitution stipulated:

The State Council shall act as a collegiate body. It shall be composed of the President, the Prime Minister and other ministers and shall decide on important national policies which come within the scope of the powers of the President. . . .

The President shall appoint the Prime Minister with the consent of the National Assembly. . . . The Ministers shall be appointed by the President. . . . No military personnel shall be appointed Prime Minister or minister unless he has resigned from active service.

The Constitution then enumerated the matters which had to be referred to the State Council for decision; these included most of the executive powers: fundamental plans and policies on state affairs; foreign policy; proposed constitutional amendments; bills and proposed orders of the President; budgets and other financial matters; the calling of extraordinary sessions of the National Assembly; the declaration of a state of siege; military affairs; appointment and removal of justices of the Supreme Court, the Prosecutor General, the Chairman of the Board of Audit, the President of the National Universities, ambassadors and ministers, and the chief of staff of each of the armed forces; and other matters presented by the Prime Minister or other ministers.[37] Decisions in the State Council, which could not contain more than fifteen or less than eight members, were to be made by majority vote, with the President "authorized to vote and to break a tie vote." [38]

In this State Council, a curious mixture of presidential and responsible cabinet forms of government appeared.[39] The President's power to appoint the Prime Minister with the consent of the legislature seemed, at first glance, to be merely the naming of the majority party's or majority coalition's choice. It could mean, however, that the President might propose a candidate on his own initiative—particularly since the power of removal of the Prime Minister was to be exercised by the President with no reference to legislative concurrence. Once the Prime Minister was appointed, it would appear that he would be as susceptible to presidential as to legislative control in the exercise of the "power of the President." Given the fact that no constitutional provision was made for the dissolution of the National Assembly in case of disagreement with the Prime Minister and his cabinet, the legislature could not exercise continuing control over the cabinet in case of disagreement. At best, the legislature could fail to pass the State Council's program, which would result in deadlock.

Article 57 was the familiar emergency clause, similar to Article 48 of the old Weimar Constitution:

When in time of civil war, in a dangerous situation arising from foreign relations, in case of natural calamity or on account of a grave economic or financial crisis, it is necessary to take urgent measures for the maintenance of public order and security, the President shall have the power to issue orders having the effect of law or to take necessary financial disposition, provided, however, that the President shall exclusively exercise such power if time is lacking for convening of the National Assembly.

The second paragraph of the article, however, hedged against arbitrary use of this power.

Such orders or dispositions shall be reported without delay to the National Assembly for confirmation. If confirmation of the National Assembly is not obtained, such orders or dispositions shall lose their effect thereafter and the President shall promulgate such non-confirmation without delay.

For the new Korean Republic to meet the future without some machinery for rapid executive decisions would have been ignoring the realities of the situation. Whether the emergency clause would destroy the "democratic" system in

Korea, however, only time could tell. It was a strong weapon entrusted in the hands of those who were to wield the executive powers of the new government, particularly the first President of the Republic, who would establish precedents in the exercise of his emergency powers.

Though the constitutional framework, at first glance, appeared to establish legislative supremacy, close examination disclosed many opportunities for it to be a strong presidential form.[40] Many Koreans voiced their apprehension that the new constitutional framework was sowing the seeds for an authoritarian regime. Some powers normally found in the legislature were to be exercised by the executive as presidential powers, and the President was to share in the policy-making process of the legislature. Therefore, much depended on the first President of the Republic in establishing a democratic procedure or pattern for the new government. According to a commentator: "The Constitution has provisions which could evolve into government by a strong man or a strong party. If the international situation permits this constitution to endure, future political experiences will disclose its true nature." [41]

As to the judicial branch of the new government, Chapter V of the Constitution provided that judges should be free from legislative and executive interference. Theoretically, the judiciary was to be a check on the executive. In practice, however, the Chief Justice of the Supreme Court, appointed by the President, and judges of other courts, also appointed for a relatively short ten-year period, were amenable to presidential direction. Questions involving the constitutionality of laws were to be decided by a constitutional committee presided over by the Vice-President of the Republic and composed of five justices of the Supreme Court and five members of the National Assembly. A two-thirds majority of the committee was necessary to declare a law unconstitutional.

The chapter on "local autonomous organizations" provided for the establishment of home rule, within limitations, by national ordinance. Key functions such as police and public works would be administered from Seoul, however, while local organizations would merely "manage their property and perform their administration within the framework of laws and orders and shall perform additional tasks as are delegated to them by law."

The procedure for amending the Constitution was specified in Chapter IX:

A motion to amend the Constitution shall be introduced by either the President or by one-third or more of the members of the National Assembly duly elected and seated.

Proposed amendments to the Constitution shall be announced by the President to the public. . . . The decision on the amendment to the Constitution requires the concurrence of more than two-thirds of the members of the National Assembly duly elected and seated.

It is evident that a considerable degree of differentiation of governmental roles and structures was established by the Constitution. Whether the various branches and organs of the government could function and develop autonomously, with an optimum degree of coordination and integration among them, could be ascertained only after the governmental system had begun its operation. The processes for formally amending the Constitution were not the most difficult, in terms of the requirements for amendment. It was obviously hoped that the constitutional system would prove versatile and adaptable.

As one of its first acts under the new Constitution, the National Assembly elected the Republic's first President, Syngman Rhee, and Vice-President, Yi Si-yŏng, on July 20, 1948, and both were inaugurated on July 24. The Republic of

Korea was officially proclaimed on the third anniversary of V-J Day, thus ending the three-year administration of South Korea by the United States military government. The Supreme Commander of the Allied Powers, General MacArthur, in his speech at the inauguration of the Republic, declared that the birth of the Republic meant "liberty reborn" and that "nothing [would] prevent" the Korean people from being "free men of a free nation." [42]

Chapter 2

The Republic in Operation

Although the Korean people were exhorted to be "free men of a free nation," such freedom awaited substantiation as the Republic was inaugurated amid pomp and fanfare. Whether or not the democratic orientation of the Constitution and the institutional framework of a representative government would actually bring political freedom remained to be seen. Only time could tell if the Koreans, who had little or no experience historically with a representative government, would be capable of developing democratic processes in the operation of republican institutions.

Some astute observers had the nagging apprehension that many Koreans were still "living with the mental heritage of the Yi Dynasty," [1] the last indigenous political system, although the superstructure of the reborn state was that of a republic. These observers feared that Korea was a republic at the top but a dynasty at the base. The question, then, was in which direction the Republic would actually develop. The character of the Rhee regime was to be crucial at such an epoch-making juncture, because the regime would be setting the whole governmental organization into motion and establishing precedents in most areas.

The Character of the Rhee Regime

The first political task, of course, was the formation of the government. Although the election of Dr. Rhee as the President of the Republic was little more than a formality—with only thirteen votes cast for Kim Ku—the election of Yi Si-yŏng was not as simple. In the voting for Vice-President, 197 assemblymen were present and no candidate received the necessary two-thirds of the votes on the first ballot. On the second ballot, Yi was elected with 133 votes, and 62 votes were cast for Kim Ku, who had vehemently and publicly opposed the formation of a "separate" government in South Korea. This fact indicated, among other things, that at least a third of the assemblymen were casting their votes not on the basis of careful political judgment but for a recognized political figure. Kim's views and conspicuous opposition to the "separate" government had made him totally unacceptable to Rhee as Vice-President; in fact, Kim was Rhee's most formidable rival.

Rhee was willing to have Yi in the vice-presidential position. It was a known fact, however, that Yi had been a follower of Kim Ku since their period of exile in China. In this sense, the Rhee-Yi team was a "coalition" between the two exile groups that had returned to Korea from the United States and from China. Yi, however, could hardly be a rival to Rhee, considering Yi's advanced age and failing health, his somewhat awkward manners, and his political and even physical stature. Yi was vastly different from Kim, who was robust, well-known, and possessed a charismatic magnetism for a large segment of the population, particularly the rural people.

Personality clashes and political rivalries could be also seen in the choice of Prime Minister. Rhee's first choice was Yi

Yun-yŏng, a Methodist minister and acting chairman of the Chosŏn Democratic Party, composed largely of North Korean refugees residing in South Korea. Yi Yun-yŏng would have been amenable to Rhee, also a Methodist, both in public and in private, but he was emphatically rejected by the Assembly, 132 to 59. The leader of the Hanguk Democratic Party, Kim Sŏng-su, was supported by a large group in the Assembly, but Rhee refused to accept him. A compromise was reached in the selection of Yi Pŏm-sŏk. He was a former official of the provisional government exiled in China, and, since his return to Korea, head of a militaristic "youth movement," the Korean National Youth Corps. Some observers noticed similarities between this youth corps and the Hitler Jugend.[2]

The new cabinet represented varying groups, but observers noted that it was not particularly strong.[3] It was inevitably composed largely of inexperienced political appointees. Criticism was immediately directed against the new cabinet on the score that it was overwhelmingly "southern"—that is, drawn from southern families—although many prominent "northern" refugees were available. Furthermore, Rhee obviously could not appoint adherents of the views of Kim Ku and Kim Kyu-sik, who refused to recognize the legitimacy of the "separate" government in South Korea. The cabinet members, therefore, were chosen from a narrowly limited ground, and the Korean people were generally unimpressed with the appointments for one reason or the other.[4] The appointments were quickly dubbed "child's play" and the cabinet was rated "third class."[5]

As a politician, President Rhee saw his first task to be that of consolidating his regime. Rhee knew that he faced opposition from a number of directions and that his administration had to cope with a divergence of views. Whether Korean politics would develop in a "liberal" direction was to depend on how these tasks would be accomplished by the first all-Korean government, and particularly by Rhee.

In the early months of his administration, Rhee appeared to scrutinize his appointees for any tendency to develop an independent following within the administration and outside it. Within months of taking office, he initiated the first of the cabinet shake-ups which were to become a hallmark of his administration. Any cabinet minister who had shown any indication that he was politically unreliable from Rhee's standpoint was immediately dismissed. Similarly, any minister who would not readily agree with Rhee at cabinet meetings or in private was abruptly removed.[6] If Rhee's original appointments had been uninspiring, some of those that followed were even more so.[7]

Under these conditions, few cabinet ministers dared argue with Rhee or even make any positive suggestions. Virtually all decisions in both policy and administrative matters were made by the President himself—the beginning of a vicious circle in which Rhee quickly became so occupied with trivia that he was unable to supervise an orderly process of decision-making. The presidency became overloaded with problems, many of which could have been far more effectively and promptly handled by various ministries.

Few criticized Rhee for these practices. The Prime Minister, who was appointed with the consent of the Assembly, was the only one in the cabinet who could have checked them. The Prime Minister, however, chose to remain docile to Rhee. In the first few months of the Rhee administration, therefore, what may be called a "personalism," as opposed to "institutionalism," was established in the Republic headed by Rhee, who was to become bigger than the entire institution of the Korean government. The differentiation of governmental

roles and structures that were constitutionally established proceeded at a snail's pace.

Meanwhile, the Communists in North Korea had organized
and trained a sufficient number of troops to harass periodically
the border guards of South Korea. At the same time that these
sporadic raids kept the South Korean authorities uncomfort-
able, the government had to cope with a full-scale mutiny in
the south only a few weeks after the establishment of the
Republic. On the night of October 19, 1948, an army regi-
ment, which was to be dispatched to Cheju Island to subjugate
Communist-inspired rebels, mutinied in the town of Yŏsu on
the southwestern tip of Korea. Evidently led by leftist elements, the insurgents won over a large segment of the civilian
population by urging revenge against the oppressive local police, many of whom were holdovers from the hated Japanese
occupation.[8] Spreading rumors that all Korea had fallen to the
rebels, the insurgents marched to capture the nearby town of
Sunch'ŏn. Here, however, loyal troops checked the advance
and dealt summary punishments to the rebels; government
troops entered Yŏsu by the end of October.

Predictably, the Yŏsu-Sunch'ŏn rebellion gave a great im-
petus to the open suppression of civil liberties in South Korea.
The political and cultural environment was becoming suspicious, intolerant, and oppressive. Rumors of imminent invasion
from the North were widespread, while only the lightly
armed police, with numerous holdovers from the Japanese
period, were unquestionably loyal to the government. Government spokesmen estimated that two thousand persons had
been killed in the uprisings; it later turned out that 1,002
persons actually died.[9] During the first week of November,
approximately seven hundred persons, including many prominent figures of varied persuasions, had been arrested by the
police for political reasons. A law regulating press activities

was passed in November which made disturbances of the tranquility of the state a criminal offense.[10]

It was subsequently reported to the United Nations Commission that 89,710 arrests were made between September 4, 1948, and April 30, 1949. Of those arrested, 28,404 persons were released, 21,606 were turned over to the prosecutor's office for further proceedings, 29,284 were transferred to a "security office," 6,985 were transferred to the military police, and 1,187 cases were pending.[11]

In Seoul, the chief of police had walls and bulletin boards plastered with a proclamation asserting that the "North Korea's People's Army had already begun its invasion of South Korea" and that persons inciting disturbances would be shot on sight. On December 7, Minister of Education An Ho-sang ordered the directors of all educational institutions to file detailed personal histories of their teachers. The Minister stated that "teachers who are communists or inclined to the left or who do not make their beliefs clear will be excluded from any position in the educational field." [12]

President Rhee now manifested profound interest in establishing effective control over the police and the armed forces and in cultivating personal loyalty to himself among the officers of the police and the armed forces. High police and army officers were carefully and confidentially rescreened. Anyone who was suspected of leftist tendencies or disloyalty to the President was dismissed under one pretext or the other, while Rhee showed the rest of the police and army chieftains his special favor and "generosity." Many of the high-ranking police and army officers were those who had served under the Japanese rule without nationalist scruples; they were happy to remain in their privileged positions and to serve the new master who favored them. With the open courting of the President himself, these police and army officers were to become important groups of the new elite class of the Republic. A survey of Korean newspapers for this period shows that Rhee had been quite frequently and conspicuously photographed together with high-ranking army and police officers, usually at a presidential presentation of decorations or citations.

The fact that South Korea's leftists had been ruthlessly driven underground at the cost of severe curtailment of civil liberties in no way inhibited political bickering on the right. Although Rhee's conservative opponents were as anti-Communist as he, this fact did not produce political harmony. In fact, the absence of significant ideological differences tended to encourage rather than inhibit quarrels over minor issues, as did Rhee's penchant for branding any opponent as pro-Communist or traitor.

Since the first "Constitutional Assembly" was to serve for two years, new elections were scheduled for 1950. Although Rhee's followers represented the largest single bloc in the Assembly, they faced an uncertain future. After all, they still occupied only a third of the seats and had naturally become associated with numerous harsh and quite unpopular policies and executive measures. In March, 1949, Rhee suddenly proposed that the 1950 elections be postponed.[13] This move, however, quickly encountered stiff opposition from within Korea and without, including the American government, which had been a prime mover in establishing the Republic.

Until this time, few Koreans dared openly challenge President Rhee's position. There remained, however, one political leader who was not awed by Rhee. The aging and austere Kim Ku had lived in political eclipse since his unsuccessful opposition to the "separate" elections, and since then had heard himself, ailing Kim Kyu-sik, and their followers denounced by Rhee's supporters as "blind men" who were "baited by the Communists." Kim Ku was one of the few who vocally criticized the American policies in Korea that had led to the "separate" government and who denounced the Rhee regime.[14] Because he had been president of the exiled Korean Provisional Government and due to his stand on national unification, Kim retained a considerable following among the Korean Independence Party and other rightist groups. Since 1950 elections were anticipated and many assemblymen were becoming weary of Dr. Rhee, Kim Ku's name figured prominently in their minds.

On June 24, 1949, a South Korean army lieutenant, claiming to be a member of the Korean Independence Party, was admitted to Kim Ku's study, where he shot and almost instantly killed the old "independence fighter." President Rhee termed the assassination "unfortunate and shocking," but later issued another statement that "fact will show that Mr. Kim Ku's death was the direct result of divergence of opinion within his own party." [15] Rhee further stated that "though these clashes of views were never known to the public, one of Mr. Kim's followers decided to put an end to these clashes." [16] On July 2, however, the military police arrested the editor of a Seoul daily for printing the statement of a Korean Independence Party spokesman that police reports concerning the assassin's motives did not agree with evidence uncovered by the party's investigators. In any case, Dr. Rhee's most prominent political rival was thus permanently eliminated.

While the Rhee government continued to stress the danger of Communist invasion and internal subversion, the United States government officially took issue with Rhee over two matters: the administration's stated intention to postpone the Assembly elections scheduled for May, 1950, and the failure to act vigorously against inflation in South Korea. In an *aide-mémoire* to the Korean ambassador to the United States, Secretary of State Dean Acheson voiced the United States government's "concern" over the reported intention of the Korean government to postpone the elections. Acheson declared

that the United States aid, both military and economic, to the Republic of Korea has been predicated upon the existence and growth of democratic institutions within the Republic. Free, popular elections, in accordance with the constitution and other basic laws of the Republic, are the foundation of those democratic institutions.[17]

In exceptionally blunt terms, Secretary Acheson was officially declaring that democracy must not only exist but also grow in Korea. The American government was threatening the Rhee administration that unless democratic elections were held as scheduled, the United States aid program might be seriously reviewed. Since the continued existence of the infant republic was almost entirely dependent on the continuance of the American aid, the United States government was telling Rhee that an undemocratic Korea, or an undemocratic regime in it, was unworthy of survival.

Acheson also threatened to review the entire Korean aid program unless vigorous anti-inflationary measures were forthcoming. The *aide-mémoire* continued: "It is the judgment of this Government that the financial situation in Korea has already reached critical proportions and that, unless this progressive inflation is curbed in the none too distant future, it cannot but seriously impair Korea's ability to utilize effectively the economic assistance" [18] provided by the United States. With the existence of the Republic threatened, President Rhee declared that elections should be held on schedule and that taxes would be raised as an anti-inflationary measure. Political and administrative demands were made by the United States government and these demands were met by the Ko-

rean government. This unique relationship prompted observers to make the following comments:

In few areas of the world is American prestige more closely tied
to the internal developments of a foreign state. Whether justified
or not, the United States will be held responsible for what happens in Korea.[19]

Meanwhile, it was quite obvious that President Rhee was
not at all anxious to hold elections. He had openly split with
the Hanguk Democratic Party the previous year over issues
of patronage and a number of policy matters; the Hanguk
Democrats had charged him with ingratitude for the support
they had given him in winning the presidency in 1948. In
February, 1949, the Hanguk Democratic Party had merged
with other conservative elements to form the anti-Rhee Democratic Nationalist Party.[20] Independents on the political
scene, now appalled by the excesses of Rhee's campaign against
the domestic left and also by the general executive usurpation
of the prerogatives of the legislature, tended to favor some
effective check on the executive. A major fight was imminent.

The Democratic Nationalist Party, which spearheaded the
opposition to Rhee, decided to take concrete measures to
emasculate Rhee's position. As a means to this end, seventy-
nine assemblymen, mostly members of the Democratic Nationalist Party, in January, 1950, proposed an amendment to
the Constitution that had been promulgated by the Assembly
less than two years before. The proposed amendment was to
secure a clear-cut cabinet system instead of the curious mixture of presidential and cabinet systems that existed. The
amendment would make Rhee purely a ceremonial head of
the state and make it possible for the new Democratic Nationalist Party to control the cabinet.[21] President Rhee and his
followers were, of course, vehemently opposed to such a

change. The constitutional amendment was formally presented to the Assembly on March 10, but it was subsequently defeated by a vote of 79 for, 33 against, with 66 abstaining. Apparently, not enough assemblymen were convinced that they should take the drastic action of amending the Constitution so soon after its adoption. Probably, those assemblymen who opposed the constitutional amendment saw a more reasonable means of coping with Rhee—namely, defeating Rhee's followers in the May, 1950, elections and then dumping Rhee in the 1952 presidential election in the Assembly. This approach would preserve existing constitutional features.

The crucial elections were scheduled for May 30. By 1950, the division between North and South Korea had become so firmly established that all but the extreme leftists, who were in any case outlawed, decided to participate in the elections. A total of 2,237 candidates had registered for election to the 210 Assembly seats. Of these candidates, 368 belonged to parties led by President Rhee himself or directly backed by the government: the Taehan Nationalist Party, 149; the Nationalist Party, 115; the Taehan Youth Corps, 61; the Taehan Labor Union, 43. The Democratic Nationalist Party nominated 158 candidates, and the Socialist Party, 27. And 1,218 candidates, or some 55 per cent of the total, declared themselves independent of any party affiliation, again indicating that party politics had not yet come into being in Korea.[22]

About 91.9 per cent of the 8,434,737 qualified voters cast their ballots. When the election returns were tallied, the result was a resounding defeat for the Rhee administration. The Taehan Nationalist Party had 24 candidates elected, the Nationalist Society 12, the Taehan Youth Corps 11, and the Taehan Labor Union 2. Even including those who might be considered pro-administration, Rhee could count on only about 57 votes[23]—far short of a majority. Only 12 were publicly pledged to Rhee, while the Democratic Nationalists occupied 23 seats, and the independents an impressive 127.

Almost immediately following the elections, the Democratic Nationalists again set about introducing a measure to make the cabinet responsible to the Assembly. But, like Rhee, they were all too preoccupied with politics to detect the stealthy military buildup in North Korea. The Second Assembly opened its session on June 19, 1950, and the Communist army attacked South Korea six days later.

The Korean War and Political Battles

There are three types of crises in the life of a democratic nation, according to Clinton L. Rossiter; "three well-defined threats to its existence as both nation and democracy." [24] The first of these is war, particularly a war to repel invasion, when a state must convert its peacetime political and social order into a wartime fighting machine and overmatch the skill and efficiency of the enemy. The necessity of some degree of readjustment in the governmental structure and of contraction of the normal political and social liberties cannot be denied, particularly by a people faced with the grim horror of national enslavement. The second crisis is "rebellion," when the authority of a constitutional government is resisted openly by a large number of its citizens. The third crisis, according to Rossiter, is "economic depression." He holds that an economic crisis could be as direct a threat to a nation's continued and constitutional existence as war or rebellion.

Within two years following the establishment of the Korean government, the infant republic was to face all three types of crises. The economic condition in South Korea had been one of endless despair, despite sizable American economic aid.[25] The agrarian half of the divided peninsula could not even produce enough foodstuff for South Koreans and the numerous refugees from the North. The land reform measures, which were intended to improve the economic conditions of farmers, who constituted nearly three-fourths of the population, were a series of failures.[26] The Republic also faced a number of rebellions, beginning with the Yŏsu-Sunchŏn incidents of October, 1948. The South Korean police and army had to engage in prolonged subjugation campaigns against largely Communist-inspired rebels. In these campaigns, the civil liberties of countless persons were often ignored. Frequently, hapless villagers, suspected of aiding the guerrillas, were summarily executed.[27]

While South Korea was coping with these various threats to its survival, an economic and cultural agreement and "other reciprocal aid agreements" were signed in Moscow by the Soviet Union and the "Democratic People's Republic of Korea" on March 17, 1949. The informed segment of South Koreans had been feeling increasingly uneasy about the bellicose behavior of the North Korean armed units at the 38th parallel. The South Korean National Assembly resolved in a formal request addressed to the American authorities "that U.S. forces be kept in South Korea until the security forces of the Republic of Korea were capable of maintaining order." [28]

Despite this unusual request publicly made to an occupying power, Washington decided to withdraw the occupation forces from the Republic of Korea in pursuance of the recommendation contained in the United Nations General Assembly resolution of December 12, 1948, that the occupying powers should "withdraw their occupation forces from Korea as early as practicable." [29] In 1948, the United States could sway the General Assembly actions, and it was obvious that Washington was desirous of mutual and simultaneous disengagement of American and Soviet armed forces from the Korean peninsula. The United Nations Commission on Korea subsequently reported that it had verified the withdrawal of American occupation forces from Korea and that only the five hundred Americans of the Korean Military Advisory Group remained. The commission then notified the Soviet Union of its readiness to extend the same offices of observance and verification of the withdrawal of Soviet forces, which was reportedly completed before the American withdrawal. However, the commission received no reply.

While the American troops were being withdrawn from South Korea, President Truman, in his message to Congress of June 7, 1949, on economic assistance to Korea, made a rare comment on the United States "foreign policy aims" in Korea. The President stated that the continuation of assistance was of great importance to

the successful achievement of the foreign policy aims of the United States. . . . Korea has become a testing ground in which the validity and practical value of the ideas and principles of democracy which the Republic is putting into practice are being matched against the practices of Communism which have been imposed upon the people of North Korea. The survival and progress of the Republic toward a self-supporting, stable economy will have an immense and far-reaching influence on the people of Asia. Such progress by the young Republic will encourage the people of southern and southeastern Asia and the islands of the Pacific to resist and reject the communist propaganda with which they are besieged. Moreover, the Korean Republic, by demonstrating the success and tenacity of democracy in resisting communism, will stand as a beacon to the people of northern Asia in resisting the control of the communist forces which have overrun them.[30]

A President of the United States, in an official communication to Congress, had thus characterized the Republic of Korea as a testing ground of democracy that should stand as a beacon to all peoples of Asia. Having flatly stated that the ideals and principles of democracy were being put into practice in the Republic, President Truman declared in effect that helping the Republic survive and develop as a showcase of the success and tenacity of democracy was a foreign policy aim of the United States.

Korea had received a total of 181.2 million dollars in American economic and military aid from 1946 to 1948; [31] President Truman, in his message to Congress, requested that the appropriation be raised to 150 million dollars for the fiscal year 1950. Furthermore, a military defense agreement and a formal agreement concerning the already existing Korean Military Advisory Group was signed and came into force in January, 1950. It was not unlikely that the South Korean Republic would become a viable entity—given time.

Suddenly, on a Sunday morning, June 25, 1950, almost exactly one year after the completion of the withdrawal of American troops from Korea, the heavily armed Communist army of North Korea launched a full-scale invasion of South Korea across the 38th parallel. South Korean defenses, caught by complete surprise and outmatched from the beginning by the far superior fire power and mobility of the Communist army, collapsed with frightening rapidity. President Rhee urgently cabled a plea to President Truman:

Beginning in early morning 25 June, North Korean Communist Army began armed aggression against South. Your Excellency and Congress of the United States are already aware of the fact that our people, anticipating incident such as today's established strong national defense force in order to secure *bulwark of democracy in the east* and to render service to world peace. . . . As we face this national crisis, putting up brave fight, we appeal for your increasing support and ask that you at the same time extend effective and timely aid in order to prevent this act of destruction of world peace.[32]

General MacArthur's headquarters in Tokyo also sent disturbing news to Washington:

South Korean units unable to resist determined North Korean offensive. Contributory factor exclusive enemy possession of tanks and fighter planes. South Korean casualties as an index to fighting have not shown adequate resistance capabilities or the will to fight and our estimate is that complete collapse is imminent.[33]

President Truman reasoned: "There was no doubt! The Republic of Korea needed help at once if it was not to be overrun. More seriously, a Communist success in Korea would put Red troops and planes within easy striking distance of Japan, and Okinawa and Formosa would be open to attack from two sides." [34] On June 27, President Truman upset the Soviet calculation with his historic decision to extend protection to South Korea.

From Taejŏn, to which President Rhee and his entourage quickly fled in the night of June 25 without so much as giving his countrymen a warning that Seoul might be abandoned, Rhee exhorted South Koreans to drive out the invaders—to no avail. Seoul fell on June 28, only three days after the opening salvo of the invasion. Hanson Baldwin, commenting on the military situation in Korea, expressed the opinion that "the unpopularity of the Syngman Rhee government and the questionable political and military reliability of the army and police force are the greatest weakness of the defending forces." [35]

By June, 1950, the Republic of Korea had received weapons from the United States that were valued, according to the Korean historian Sin Sŏk-ho, at about 17 million dollars.[36] These weapons were barely enough to arm some 50,000 "con-

stabularies" of the Republic. At the time of the outbreak of
the war, there were eight regular divisions with some 80,000
men. Even after including 17,000 men in various units with
hardly any weapons, the total man-power was less than
100,000. The South Korean army had 60 105-millimeter can-
nons, 140 antitank guns, 27 armored cars, and 10 training
planes, but neither long-range artillery pieces nor tanks. According to Sin, the North Koreans attacked with 10 regular
divisions, 1,643 artillery pieces, 500 tanks, and 211 aircraft,
including fighter planes.

The fighting was to rage on the narrow peninsula for three
full years, and it was to cost South Korea a million lives
among civilians alone and damage estimated at three billion
dollars.[37] The United States was to suffer 157,530 casualties,
including 33,629 battle deaths. As the battle front seemed to
reach a stalemate and the armistice negotiations began in the
summer of 1951, political wars in South Korea were resumed.
With President Rhee's term due to expire in less than a year,
his political opponents continued to dominate the Assembly,
which was to elect the next President in 1952.

Determined to overthrow Rhee in the 1952 election, his
opponents in the Assembly could find numerous instances of
executive corruption and malfeasance with which to attack
the administration. The most flagrant of these was the National Defense Corps scandal. The Corps, headed by General
Kim Yun-gŭn, had been hastily organized by the government
in December, 1950, as a paramilitary unit, lest South Korean
youth fall under the control of Communists when the battle
line was pushed south again. As thousands upon thousands of
Corps members straggled south in the second evacuation of
Seoul in January, 1951, they appeared like armies of beggars,
and an untold number of them died of malnutrition and ex-
posure by the time they had walked in the bitter cold almost

half the length of the Korean Peninsula to reach southern cities. An investigation revealed that the commander of the Corps and his coterie had embezzled a large portion of the funds allocated for food, clothing, and equipment. After a much publicized military trial, five officers of the Corps, including General Kim, faced a firing squad on a sultry summer day, August 12, 1951, at the outskirts of Taegu.

Though President Rhee periodically stated that he would not be a candidate for re-election, his activities as early as the spring of 1951 belied these protestations. In April, 1951, he departed from his previous aloofness from partisan politics by directing the formation of an administration political party to be headed by himself. On August 15, the anniversary of Korea's Independence Day, Rhee publicly declared the need for a political vehicle that would be committed to support him.[38]

Rhee encouraged his supporters within the Assembly to organize a new political party and, at the same time, prodded pro-administration groups outside the Assembly to form their own party. These two groups failed to merge as a single political party. In December the Assembly group founded the Liberal Party; a second "Liberal Party" was organized by Rhee's supporters outside the legislature.[39] There existed, therefore, two "political parties" with the same name, dedicated to the proposition of supporting Rhee but divided by clashing personal ambitions among their members. President Rhee was apparently to depend on the group within the Assembly for support in the legislature and on the group outside the Assembly for demonstration of "popular support"—until the merger of these groups was accomplished. Even while the Korean War raged to the north, the party organizations were rushed to completion in the closing days of 1951.

President Rhee had two basic alternatives in his campaign

to secure re-election. One was to operate within the existing constitutional structure, and the other was to amend the Constitution to provide for direct election of the President by the people, a majority of whom still believed that Rhee was the "father of the nation."

It appeared that Rhee could bring considerable pressure to bear on the Assembly to accept him for a second term. The overriding necessity of maintaining at least a façade of national unity during wartime, for example, would argue against ousting the top leadership in the midst of the war. Even Rhee's political opponents recognized that President Rhee commanded at least the grudging respect of the United Nations Command, which directed war efforts, and that Rhee had established fairly firm control of the Korean army and police. With some effective persuasion within the Assembly, it was conceivable that Rhee's objectives might be achieved without the adverse publicity that would certainly accompany an outright constitutional amendment in the midst of war.[40]

Such a course, however, could only be a temporary expedient. It in no way checked the constitutional prerogatives of the Assembly—among other things, that of electing the President—which would presumably continue to harass his administration and to threaten the defeat of Rhee or any chosen successor four years later. In the end, President Rhee and his followers decided on seeking a positive and lasting solution to the problem. The administration introduced a constitutional amendment providing for popular election of the President and establishment of a two-house legislature. This administration move, however, was defeated in the Assembly on January 18, 1952, by an overwhelming vote of 143 to 19.

The Democratic Nationalist Party that masterminded this significant parliamentary victory lost little time in channeling this momentum into a counterdemand for a cabinet system.

By April 17, the opposition-inspired draft had the signature of 122 assemblymen who would support the move [41]—one more than two-thirds of the Assembly membership. In the face of this humiliating defeat, the Rhee administration decided to launch an all-out assault against the Assembly. Against the bloody background of the Korean War, which tended to appear strangely remote from the provisional capital city and its political preoccupations, a political war was declared in Pusan by Rhee against the Assembly. Rhee replaced the somewhat ineffectual Home Minister with the vice-chairman of the Liberal Party, Yi Pŏm-sŏk, whose National Youth Corps had grown in number and influence as a strong-arm auxiliary of the administration. Almost simultaneous with Yi's appointment, "spontaneous" mass demonstrations began. They were spearheaded by members of various "youth corps," including a group that menacingly called itself the Pekkoldan (White Skeleton Corps), which warned the assemblymen against opposing Rhee [42] and called for his re-election.

Minister Yi Pŏm-sŏk had been in office only a week when the Rhee administration initiated what has been called the period of "political undulation" or "political crisis" by imposing martial law in the Pusan area on May 26, ostensibly as a measure against guerrillas, who certainly did not exist in the area at the time. The Assembly, however, was not cowed by naked threat. By a vote of ninety-six to three—but with numerous abstentions—the Assembly voted to lift this martial law, in effect overriding Rhee's "emergency" measure, which, under the Constitution, had to be ratified by the Assembly.

The Assembly action, far from checking Rhee, only infuriated him. The Assembly building was now surrounded by the military police. On May 27, some fifty assemblymen, while they were aboard Assembly shuttle buses, were suddenly towed by army trucks to a military police station, where four of the assemblymen were jailed—although they were legally immune from arrest during Assembly session. On the following day, the administration's Office of Public Information hastily announced that "far-reaching Communist connections have been uncovered, and authorities are taking steps to make a thorough investigation." [43] It was subsequently alleged that these assemblymen had received their political funds from "international Communist organizations."

President Rhee denied the reports of intimidation and coercion against the legislators as "unfair stories and unfounded rumors." [44] Despite the demands by the Assembly to lift the martial law and a strongly worded communiqué issued by the United Nations Commission expressing deep concern about the political turmoil in Pusan, Rhee continued to wield power as though the legislators did not exist at all. Massive, "spontaneous" demonstrations, shouting slogans in support of Rhee, were organized by the government day after day in Pusan, and on May 28, shops and markets and even schools were closed down in South Korean cities to permit a four-hour demonstration for Rhee's re-election.

Within days the crisis worsened. On May 31, Home Minister Yi announced the arrest of eleven persons, including the secretary of a leading opposition assemblyman, Chang Myŏn, on charges of plotting to assassinate Rhee. According to police announcements, Assemblyman Chang, a devout Catholic who was favored by many members of the Democratic Nationalist Party to succeed Rhee as President, was working with the conspirators and making use of money provided by the Communists to depose Rhee and bring about unification negotiations with North Korea. The charges were preposterous, but to the uninformed mass of Koreans it appeared much as though Rhee was fighting valiantly against the most sinister kind of conspiracy.[45]

Meanwhile, the administration had its supporters and paid

ruffians from all over South Korea stage around-the-clock demonstrations around the Assembly building in Pusan. Finally, demonstrators from numerous Assembly constituencies completely surrounded the Assembly building and demanded the recall of "traitorous," anti-Rhee assemblymen and the dissolution of the Assembly. President Rhee now openly threatened to dissolve the Assembly if his demands were not met, observing that "the will of the people is more important than the letter of the Constitution."

More and more anti-Rhee assemblymen were arrested on one pretext or another or they were one jump ahead of Rhee's police and unable to take issue with the pro-Rhee groups. When about one hundred anti-administration legislators and political leaders attempted to hold an "anti-dictatorship" rally on June 20 in a Pusan restaurant, they were physically attacked by a pro-Rhee "mob or policemen disguised as a mob," who threw chairs, tables, flower vases, and stones at them and seriously injured several of them, including Cho Pyŏng-ok. It had been said that democracy substitutes the counting of heads for the breaking of heads. In a restaurant in Pusan, called the International Club, Rhee's followers engaged in the breaking of heads of Rhee's political opponents.

Taking advantage of the "officially manufactured popular will," [46] but above all making full use of the strong-arm resources that were monopolized by the wartime government and hired thugs under the protection of Rhee's police, the administration continued to bully the Assembly. Finally, on July 3, the unprecedented "roundup" of assemblymen by the police began. The Assembly session of the previous day had been attended by only eighty-six members, mostly of the pro-Rhee group. This figure was, of course, far short of the 123 required to amend the Constitution. From Home Minister Yi went out a stern order to the police that some sixty-five opposition assemblymen known to be either boycotting the session or in hiding in the Pusan area were to be "escorted" to the July 4 session. To obtain the quorum, the Korean National Police drew a gigantic dragnet across the Pusan area already under the martial law.

Some eighty reluctant assemblymen had been herded to the Assembly hall by midnight on July 4, and police stood guard lest any of the assemblymen should attempt to escape from the building. By dawn there were fewer than a dozen assemblymen missing, but to preclude any question of quorum, the martial law commander released on bail all but one of the legislators then supposedly on trial for "treason." The ten were dutifully marched to the Assembly hall.

The Rhee administration had thus "won" the fight against the Assembly. The Assembly debated into the night on July 5, and "a few strong voices were raised to call that day the final, brief hour of Korean democracy." [47] But it became clear to all present—some of them now being "lodged" and guarded by police in the Assembly hall for two days—that no one would be allowed out of the hall until the amendments were passed. By a lopsided vote of 163 to zero, with only three abstentions, the Assembly passed constitutional amendments which provided for:

(*a*) a direct, popular election of the President and Vice-President, (*b*) creation of an upper house, (*c*) recommendation of cabinet appointees by the Prime Minister, and (*d*) limited authorization for the National Assembly to dissolve the State Affairs Council (cabinet) by a vote of non-confidence.[48]

The legislature's capitulation was now complete and the Assembly voted the presidential and vice-presidential election laws that were proclaimed on July 18. The administration then scheduled the elections for August 5, less than twenty days later. Quite predictably, the Liberal Party on July 19 officially "nominated" Rhee for President and Yi Pŏm-sŏk for Vice-President.[49] Despite this formal "nomination" by his own party, President Rhee now decided to restrain the growing political influence of Yi, whose National Youth Corps had grown too powerful for Rhee's comfort. Only a few days before the elections, Rhee ordered, through the police organizations, that his followers switch their support from Yi to Ham T'ae-yŏng, a respected Christian layman. At eighty-one, Ham was the oldest and least ambitious of a handful of independent candidates for the vice-presidency. Both Rhee and Ham were elected by an overwhelming majority.[50]

Now that Rhee and the Liberal Party were firmly established in an unchallengeable position, for the time being anyway, opportunists flocked to Rhee's camp. "The intricate tie-up under the Rhee administration between government, financial institutions, and business" had already been "a matter of general knowledge." [51] But illicit practices now became much bolder. Businessmen knew that private fortunes could be amassed through cooperation with the Rhee government and its ruling Liberal Party. Political power and connections could be used not only for the acquisition of government-controlled foreign aid funds at favorable rates, but also for purchasing government-owned property at a fraction of its value, "borrowing" from the government without being pressed for repayment, and for evading the payment of taxes. Now that the authoritarian Rhee regime did not have to worry about any effective check, corruption became more and more rampant.[52] One result was that the Liberal Party was far better financed and staffed than any collection of opposing factions.

By the time the Korean truce agreement was signed in a wooden hut in P'anmunjŏm in July, 1953, the war had consumed an estimated four million lives, military and civilian, in the South and the North.[53] The entire country was devastated, with the only exception of the Taegu and Pusan areas; the 150-odd miles of battle-line, with as many as two million men on both sides, had swept across the narrow peninsula as often as four times in parts of central Korea. The southern side of the battle front was manned by troops from seventeen nations under the United Nations banners, and the northern side by soldiers of two Communist regimes. Yet, at the end, the country remained divided and the results of the war were indecisive for both sides.

Only in the arena of political battles in Pusan had there emerged a victor and a victorious party—President Rhee and the Liberal Party. The political position of Dr. Rhee was now unchallengeable and the Liberal Party was the only political machinery in South Korea that was well financed, powerful, and growing. None would deny that Dr. Rhee and his Liberal Party owed much to wartime conditions for their political victory.

The war power and the emergency power of the President were utilized to the fullest extent to bolster the political position of Rhee and his followers; yet none dared refuse these powers to Rhee because there was a war and an emergency. In the name of freedom from threatened Communist domination, a host of democratic freedoms for the South Koreans was quickly discarded. The United States, which had officially declared through the Acheson *mémoire* its commitment to "the existence and growth of democratic institutions within the Republic," was preoccupied with the expedients of war. By the time the war to defend "the bastion of democracy in the Far East" was over, many of the democratic rights of the Korean people were given crippling blows.

In 1950, President Rhee was extremely reluctant to hold

Assembly elections and had to be pressured into it by various groups in Korea as well as the United States government. In 1954, however, Rhee's opposition groups were so humiliated and disorganized that Rhee was confident of readily carrying the elections. The administration announced on April 9 that the elections would be held on May 20. President Rhee had indicated on April 6 that the administration would propose a new series of amendments to the Constitution soon after the elections.

Even before the President announced the exact contents of amendments he wished to have adopted, the Liberal Party members resolved on April 8 that the party would unconditionally "obey" the policies of the chairman, Dr. Rhee, and also that the party would endorse only those candidates for the elections who would unconditionally support the constitutional amendments to be proposed by the administration.[54] Subsequently, in a political refinement hitherto unheard of in Korea,[55] the Liberal Party nominated one candidate for each Assembly district, while the undisciplined opposition and independent candidates often ran against one another. Candidates nominated by the Liberal Party were given almost complete assistance by the treasuries of the now affluent Liberal Party, the National Police, and youth organizations, while the same groups often terrorized the opposition candidates.

About 91.1 per cent of 8,466,509 qualified voters participated in the elections. Predictably, the Liberal Party won an overwhelming victory by securing 114 seats against 15 for the Democratic Nationalist Party and 67 for assorted independents. For the first time in the stormy history of the Republic, there was a majority from one political party in the Assembly. The consolidation of President Rhee's position was all but complete.

The administration proposed on September 6 a long series

of constitutional amendments—some thirty provisions.[56] Some of the numerous provisions were to be subsequently eliminated and many others to be revised. The more important provisions, whose political significance was far-reaching, attempted, first, to eliminate the two-term restriction on presidential tenure—an obvious reflection of Rhee's desire for life tenure[57]—and, secondly, to give Korean voters the right to recall legislators by petition. Given the relative political immaturity of a large majority of Korean voters, this second provision would dangle a sword over the head of every legislator, since the administration and the ruling party could "rustle up a recall petition almost on a moment's notice."[58] A third provision proposed to abolish the post of Prime Minister, which Rhee had regarded with mistrust, especially since his experience with Yi Pŏm-sŏk, whose National Youth Corps had grown rapidly while Yi occupied the position.

Although the administration utilized every conceivable tactic in the Assembly in support of the proposed amendments, when the amendments came to vote on November 27, 1954, it turned out that the administration had suffered an agonizing defeat. With 136 votes required for a two-thirds majority, the administration had fallen one vote short. The presiding officer, Ch'oe Sun-ju of the Liberal Party, officially declared the amendments defeated.

Immediately thereafter, principal members of the Liberal Party met in an emergency strategy session. Yi Ki-bung sided with a mathematician who held that fractional votes could be rounded off to the previous whole number in tallying the votes. They claimed that since there were 203 assemblymen, only 135 votes—not 135.33 votes—were required to have two-thirds majority. As soon as the Assembly convened three days later, the same presiding officer announced that there had been a mistake in determining the requisite number of votes on the amendment bill, and the amendment bill had obtained the necessary two-thirds majority. Opposition legislators screamed their protest and walked out of the Assembly; but the "tyranny of majority" now prevailed.[59] The amendments provided for:

(*a*) removal of restrictions on re-election of the President holding office at the time of the promulgation of the Constitution, (*b*) national referendum on constitutional amendments, (*c*) abolition of the office of the Prime Minister and casting of non-confidence votes *en bloc* against the State Affairs Council, (*d*) succession to the Office of the President by the Vice-President in case of vacancy in the office of the President during the remaining period of the term, (*e*) amendment of economic provisions of the Constitution, and (*f*) authority for the House of Representatives to adopt a resolution of non-confidence against any number of the State Council.[60]

With the "passage" of a constitutional amendment that made it possible for Rhee to be re-elected for an unlimited number of terms, with the opposition completely humiliated to make the Assembly submissive to Rhee, with the abolition of the office of the Prime Minister, and with the police and army loyal to Rhee, his position became almost Caesaristic.

Chapter 3

Autocracy and the Student Uprising

For the May, 1956, presidential election, the opposition groups nominated Shin Ik-hi for President and Chang Myŏn for Vice-President, more or less representing, respectively, the "Old Guard Faction" and the "New Faction" of the Democratic Party, the former Hanguk Democratic Party.[1] The final outcome of the 1956 contest appeared a foregone conclusion on the basis of the two previous elections. Those who assumed the inevitability of a complete victory for the Liberal Party, however, calculated without the appeal of the opposition party campaign to the masses, who had been suffering from extreme economic depression, police suppression, and humiliating treatment by arrogant Liberal Party members. The opposition candidates turned out to be vigorous campaigners. They stumped the country, bitterly criticizing the administration and Liberal Party for its rampant corruption, its maladministration, and its most evident failure to better the lot of the people. "We can't make a living; so let's change!" was a slogan of the Democratic Party.

Then the opposition party lost its standard bearer practically on the eve of the election. Shin Ik-hi was en route by train to a southwestern province after addressing a huge rally attended by about 300,000 on the banks of the Han River [2] when he complained of pains in his chest and collapsed. Rushed to a hospital, he died on May 5 of a heart attack only ten days before the election—too late for the party to nominate and register another opposition candidate under the Korean election laws.

The death of Shin Ik-hi was not forgotten, however, when the voters went to the polls. Out of a total of 9.1 million votes, nearly 1.9 million "invalid" ballots were cast, most of which represented "protest" votes against the Rhee administration and "posthumous" votes for the dead opposition candidate. Nearly 2.2 million votes were also cast for Cho Bong-am, by now Rhee's old nemesis and his only living opponent.[3] Some of these votes undoubtedly would have gone to Shin, had he lived. Consequently, Rhee won only 56 per cent of the vote, compared to 72 per cent in the wartime election of 1952.

The vice-presidential race was even more noteworthy. As the votes were tallied, it soon became apparent that Chang Myŏn was running up large majorities in the cities and that even in rural areas, where the coercive measures of the police had been more effective than in urban centers, Yi Ki-bung was barely holding his own. The sole Democratic candidate for Vice-President was winning about forty-six per cent of the vote, and with pro-administration ballots divided among Yi and three maverick Liberals, Chang appeared on his way to victory. One nagging question on almost everyone's mind then was: Would the Rhee administration permit the election of an opposition Vice-President?

In Taegu, South Korea's third largest city, mysterious power failures at the counting places were followed by the entrance of Liberal Party members and the disappearance of ballot boxes. Vote counters were alleged to have invalidated large numbers of Democratic votes. As Yi Ki-bung's total began to swell, the Democrats saw their victory slipping away. Tension ran high as counting was resumed and then halted again.

On the afternoon of May 19, however, after being urged by many political leaders to accept the inevitable, President Rhee announced: "Since the will of the people has been reflected in the elections, I will carry out my duty." [4] This strangely vague statement signaled the continuation of the counting of ballots in Taegu. When the counting was completed, Chang had received over 4 million votes against 3.8 million for Yi. Chang, the opposition candidate, was now the Vice-President-elect.

Many commentators observed that the 1956 election was a partial victory of the people against the oppressive government and the Liberal Party. One wrote:

Through the May 15 presidential election, we have proven that the Korean people are capable of rational judgment, of resisting pressure from the ruling group. . . . At the same time, we have seen the ruling clique resorting to every means to prolong its own political life. [5]

The elections not only established the Democratic Party as a major political power but created a situation in which the Liberal Party could be constitutionally driven out of power, should Rhee die prior to 1960, since the Constitution provided that in such an event the Vice-President should become President for the remainder of the term. Above all, the elections dramatized the rapidly ebbing popularity of the Liberal Party, and it became apparent to Yi Ki-bung and his party colleagues that Yi's defeat could only be reversed by use of the most drastic measures in 1960.

Predictably, Chang Myŏn as the Vice-President quickly discovered that he was to receive the iciest treatment from

President Rhee. "The only official function he was allowed to perform was the collection of his salary. The senate, over which he was to have presided, remained unelected." [6]

The political lull that marked the Korean scene after the 1956 elections abruptly came to an end in 1958. In the Assembly elections of May 2, the Democrats had scored remarkable gains and raised their total number of seats from 47 to 79. The Liberals lost 5 of their seats but still retained 126, and there were 28 independents. Occupying at least one-third of the seats, the Democrats could block any more government-sponsored constitutional amendments. According to a commentator, "it was hoped that this opposition group in the Assembly would now constitute a bastion of democracy in Korea." [7]

Another quite significant fact was that the Democrats did extremely well in urban centers, where the electorates were relatively sophisticated and the coercive measures of the Liberal Party and the police pressure could not be too open. In the large urban constituencies that could elect three or more assemblymen, the Democrats far outran the Liberals and independents (see Table 2).[8] In the 132 rural constituencies,

Table 2. Assemblymen elected from urban centers, 1958

City	Liberals	Democrats	Independents
Seoul	1	14	1
Pusan	3	7	0
Taegu	0	3	1
Inch'ŏn	0	3	0
Kwangju	1	2	0
Total	5	29	2

Source: Yun Ch'ŏn-ju, "Pujŏng sŏngŏŭi pangjŏngsik" (Formulae for Rigged Elections), *Sasangge Monthly*, VIII, no. 7 (June, 1960), 112.

where an Assembly district elected one assemblyman, the Liberal Party elected 82 of its candidates against 29 Democrats. A most striking comparison could be made between the capital city of Seoul and Kangwŏn province, the backwoods region of South Korea. Both Seoul Special City and Kangwŏn province, each having about the same population, could each elect eight assemblymen. From Seoul Special City, five Liberals and three Democrats were elected in 1958, while Kangwŏn province elected eight Liberals and no Democrats.[9]

A considerable portion of the Liberal Party members, who allowed carefully for the definite and numerous advantages with which their party went into the election, read the handwriting on the wall: Unless the trend toward the Democrats could be reversed somehow, President Rhee himself might be defeated in 1960 and the Liberal Party consigned to oblivion. The Liberals now set about obtaining the passage of legislation that would help them to carry the 1960 elections.[10]

The National Security Law

Alleging a necessity for effective legislative measures against domestic Communists, Liberal assemblymen introduced, on November 18, 1958, a new national security law with extensive revisions to the existing law of the same title.[11] The proposed revisions provided for death sentences or heavy prison terms for vague crimes such as "disseminating Communist propaganda." Such a provision could obviously be adapted to election campaigns.

Opposition groups led by Cho Pyŏng-ok attacked the new bill strenuously as a transparent attempt to lump all criticism of the Rhee regime with Communist propaganda and as a legal device for use in the 1960 presidential elections. After the Democrats conducted a week-long sitdown strike against the bill in the Assembly, Liberals took matters into their own hands on Christmas Eve by calling three hundred policemen as "Assembly guards" to clear the opposition from the Assembly floor.[12] When numerous Democrats resisted, a fist fight again broke out and the opposition legislators—including a lady—were carried out of the hall and locked in the basement by uniformed police. The Liberals remaining in the Assembly hall then passed twenty-two bills which ranged from the key provisions of the controversial security law to a bill abolishing elections for local offices.[13]

The new National Security Law, promulgated on December 26, 1958, was said to aim at supplementing "the penalties and judicial procedures applicable for associations, groups or organizations which seek to over-throw the state in violation of the national constitution and the activities for the realization of their objectives." [14] Article 2 of the law declared that anyone who detected or gathered "national secrets" or aided and abetted such acts for the purpose of "benefiting the enemy" shall be punished by the death penalty or penal servitude for life. And the "national secrets" were broadly defined in Article 4 as referring to "documents, drawings, other materials, facts or information, political, economic, social, cultural, military and otherwise, which are required to be kept secret." Furthermore, it was stipulated that those who have gathered "information on Government or public office, political parties, organizations or individuals for the purpose of benefiting the enemy" shall also be punished by death or life imprisonment.

It would be difficult indeed for any opposition member, or anyone, to discuss anything without mentioning "facts or information, political, economic, social, cultural, military and otherwise." Once the open discussion of information on government or public office, political parties, organizations, or individuals was to be punished, how could any opposition member discuss anything in an election campaign? The law also declared that anyone who had "benefited by disturbing the people's minds by openly pointing out or spreading false facts" would be punished by penal servitude for not more than five years. Virtually every word in the provision could be applied and interpreted to suit the ruling power.

Article 22, dealing with "criminal libel," stated:

(1) Anyone who had openly impaired the prestige of a constitutional organ by holding a meeting or by publishing documents, tape-recorded materials, drawings and other materials of expression . . . shall be punished by penal servitude for not more than ten years.

(2) The constitutional organ under the preceding paragraph shall be the President, the Speaker of the National Assembly and the Chief Justice.

Thus Rhee and his 1956 vice-presidential candidate, Yi Ki-bung, who was now the Speaker of the House, were legally placed above any meaningful political criticism. Any criticism of Rhee's policies and actions could now be interpreted as impairing the prestige of the presidency.

The law also authorized an immediate appeal against any decision to release anyone on bail or a writ of habeas corpus, which could mean that a wounded opposition member could rot to death in the hands of the police.[15]

Article 36 further provided that for "a cogent reason to continue investigation on the crimes" falling under the provisions of this law, the period of detention could be extended. The Security Law also stipulated that "the officers, warrant officers and sergeants of the intelligence agencies of the national armed forces may conduct investigations on civilians" who have committed any crimes falling under the provisions of this law.

With the "passage" of the National Security Law, therefore, most of the democratic civil rights so elegantly guaranteed in the Constitution of 1948 could be formally and legally
crushed.[16] The President and his paid apologists abroad, however, maintained that the new law was aimed solely at the
Communists, while the fact of the matter was that South
Korean police had, long before the "passage" of the new law,
more than ample legal authority to cope with domestic communism.

Other observers noted that the manner in which the security law was "passed" appeared to be a return to the coercive
tactics of 1952. Whatever Rhee's estimation of his political
strength was, by 1959 it was no longer his wishes alone that
counted in Korean politics. The numerous hangers-on who
rode the administration gravy train no longer shared Rhee's
assumption that he remained first in the hearts of the gullible
portion of his countrymen. Desperately they sought for a
means to insure their future for four more years or longer
by securing Rhee's re-election and the election of a Liberal
Vice-President. Obviously, Rhee was no longer using people
around him as much as these people were using him.[17]

The Liberals nominated Rhee and Yi Ki-bung again for the
presidency and vice-presidency in 1960. The Democratic
convention in February, 1960, nominated Cho Pyŏng-ok to
run against Rhee, and Chang Myŏn to attempt to succeed
himself in the vice-presidency—an all-important objective in
view of Rhee's advanced age. Once again Cho and Chang
represented the Old Guard Faction and the New Faction of
the Democratic Party, respectively.

Again, misfortunes seemed to follow the opposition presidential candidate. The campaign was scarcely under way
when Cho was taken seriously ill and sent to the United States
for hospitalization on January 29. Then, in a move that was
widely interpreted as an attempt to take advantage of Cho's

incapacitation, the administration scheduled the elections for March 15, instead of the customary date in May that avoided the busy season for farmers. Whatever the motive, the administration's action proved unnecessary. Cho died at the Walter Reed Hospital of complications resulting from an abdominal operation a full month before the election.

As in 1956, the opposition had a dead body as its presidential candidate. Unlike 1956, however, when the Liberal Party and the police greatly underestimated the extent of anti-administration feelings, the administration was now on its guard.[18]

Specific instructions were sent out by the Home Ministry to police chiefs throughout the nation specifying the exact plurality by which Dr. Rhee and Mr. Lee [Yi] were to be elected. Hundreds of thousands of pre-marked ballots accompanied these instructions, and these were dutifully stuffed into the ballot boxes on the election day. Hoodlums smashed up Democratic Party offices and beat up Democratic workers and sympathizers. In rural areas voters were compelled by the police to go to the ballots in groups of three, one of whom was an arm-banded "supervisor" whose duty was to check supposedly secret ballots before they were cast.[19]

The rigging of the elections was complete throughout South Korea. In one district of Taegu, for instance, one of the urban centers which had repeatedly voted' for the opposition in previous elections, the Liberal-dominated ballot counters were at one point reporting 5,000 votes for Yi and only 35 for Chang. Upon being advised by the governor of the Northern Kyŏngsang Province that these figures would appear too lopsided, Home Minister Ch'oe In-kyu instructed the Liberals there that the official return from Taegu should be adjusted to show 85 per cent of the votes for Rhee and 75 per cent for Yi.[20]

When all the votes were "counted" after March 15, it was

announced that there were, astonishingly, no recorded "post-humous" votes for Cho; it was claimed that Rhee won 92 per cent of the vote, and the remainder was simply termed "in-valid." But the eye-opener was the vice-presidential race. The official figures showed Yi defeating Chang by a more than suspicious figure of 8,221,000 to 1,844,000—a remarkable re-versal of their 1956 contest.

The opposition groups in the National Assembly, the only public gathering where a semblance of free speech remained, protested the elections vigorously. They charged that a num-ber of votes equal to 40 per cent of the total electorate had been fabricated and used to pad the Liberal Party vote. But there was no reason to think that this protest by the opposition assemblymen would be any more effective than any of the previous Assembly demonstrations that had marked the tor-tuous course of "democracy" in South Korea.

The Student Uprising

The crude rigging and manipulation of elections now meant that the people were denied the last legal, if only inter-mittent, channel of reflecting their political views. For a month after the election, however, the discouraged Korean people merely shrugged their shoulders. They felt unable to plan and carry out dynamic protests against the Rhee adminis-tration, if only because the Liberal Party and its supporters in every quarter of commercial and political life of the nation were all too able to invoke sanctions—and in a nation with 1,400,000 unemployed, a job was a precious commodity.[21] Thus for a month after the election the atmosphere in South Korea was one of sullen resignation and brooding.

Few persons outside the small port city of Masan, a strong-hold of opposition, had known that a riot had broken out there on election day when the public became convinced that a fair election was impossible.[22] In breaking up the demonstration with tear gas and gun fire, the police killed at least seven people and injured seventy-two. Several were missing afterwards, and it was believed that the police might have hidden their bodies in order to lessen the death count. Despite separate "investigations" of the incident made by the National Assembly and the Home Ministry, no action was taken against the policemen.

The people of Masan felt suffocating fury but they were helpless against the reinforced police units. Then, on April 11, a fisherman discovered the body of Kim Chu-yŏl, a nineteen-year-old high school boy who proved to be one of the missing persons. The boy had a tear-gas shell imbedded in one eye.[23] With this discovery, all Masan went out of control; police stations, the Liberal Party building, and other public buildings were wrecked, and the local police chief was nearly killed. The people's anger had finally reached the exploding point.

Sympathetic demonstrations, nonviolent at the beginning as they were started by university students in Seoul, spread to every major city of South Korea. According to an official report, there were eighteen universities, thirty-six four-year colleges, and five junior colleges in South Korea, enrolling a total of 85,920 students as of April, 1959, a year before the massive demonstrations.[24] An estimated total of middle school and high school students in 1,706 schools was 800,000 in 1960. Potentially, over a million young people could protest against the Rhee regime.

Ministers of Justice and Home Affairs jointly issued a predictable statement blaming "devilish hands of the Communists" for disturbances throughout South Korea. President Rhee himself announced on April 16 an assertion that the Masan riots were the work of Communist agents.[25]

Students in Seoul quietly planned a series of peaceful

demonstrations in sympathy with their fellow students of Masan. Some three thousand students of Koryŏ University staged, on April 18, the first student demonstration in Seoul. As these students were returning to their campuses in response to an appeal from University President Yu Chin-o, over one hundred thugs, presumably hired by the Liberals, set upon them and in no time wounded forty students and six newspaper reporters before they dispersed.[26] This bloody incident was a match thrown into a powder keg.

When a wave of over three thousand students surged to the road leading to the presidential mansion shortly after noon on April 19, they found the way barricaded by police. Student spokesmen claimed that they wanted only to present a petition to President Rhee. But the police ordered them to disperse at once. The demonstrators continued to stampede toward the presidential mansion after crushing two barricades. The police fired tear-gas shells. The angry crowd became angrier and pressed forward. Police then fired volley after volley into the milling students.[27]

Enraged students now turned to other targets. They burned five police stations in Seoul, sacked the offices of the administration organ *Seoul Shinmun*, and broke into the Seoul Liberal Party headquarters. In many areas of the city, there was little opposition to the youthful rioters, who numbered about one hundred thousand persons, including numerous citizens who joined them by midday. Many policemen simply fled their posts, took off their uniforms, and went into hiding. But some policemen and pro-administration hoodlums brutally beat up isolated groups of young students in some areas of the city.

This was the "Righteous Uprising of April 19," or the "Student Uprising," or the "Student Revolution." Throughout the city, there were 125 dead and over 1,000 wounded.[28] Characteristically, President Rhee declared martial law and made it retroactive to the moment when the police guarding his mansion fired against the demonstrators. Heavily armed soldiers were moved into Seoul.

President Rhee had just taken the ultimate military measures when he found his position challenged from an unexpected source. In the afternoon of April 19, the United States Secretary of State, Christian A. Herter, called in the Korean ambassador to the United States, You Chan Yang (Yang Yuch'an), for a meeting. On the very same day, possibly before a message from Ambassador Yang sent to Seoul was decoded and reached President Rhee, the director of the Office of News of the State Department read a statement to correspondents:

Ambassador Yang was informed that this Government believes that the demonstrations in Korea are a reflection of public dissatisfaction over the conduct of the recent elections and repressive measures unsuited to a free democracy.[29]

This was a forceful and categorical refutation of a statement, made only three days earlier by President Rhee and echoed by Ambassador Yang himself, that the turbulence in Korea was the "work of Communist agents." The State Department spokesman continued:

The Secretary suggested that the Korean government should, in its own best interest and in order to restore public confidence, take necessary and effective action aimed at protecting democratic rights of freedom of speech, of assembly and of the press, as well as preserving the secrecy of the ballot and preventing unfair discrimination against political opponents of a party in power.

At the crucial moment of the "Student Uprising," the United States government once again—as it had through Secretary Dean Acheson in 1950—made its position emphatically clear in defense of the "democratic rights" of the Korean people. Secretary Herter justified this public position on the basis that the United States "has, in the eyes of the world, always been closely associated with Korea as a friend, supporter, and ally." [30]

The United States government thus chose to be "a friend, supporter, and ally" of the Korean people—who were then demonstrating against the Rhee regime. The Voice of America and U.S. armed forces radio stations in Korea repeatedly broadcast the content of the State Department statement, and the impact of this communication was immediate. As the American ambassador to Korea, Walter P. McConaughy, drove toward the presidential mansion on the night of April 19, the milling crowds recognized his limousine, immediately cleared a path for him, and enthusiastically cheered him. [31]

American officials in Korea remained silent in public. Many observers believe, however, that the Americans there played a quiet but significant role in furthering the cause of anti-administration demonstrators, students joined by citizenry. The United Nations Command in Korea, which had been led by General Carter B. Magruder of the United States, had tactical control of the Korean Army. The U.N. Command allowed the Martial Law Command of the Korean Army the use of tanks—but without live ammunition. [32]

By now the hated police force that had been loyal to Rhee had been demoralized; the army under the martial law commander, Lieutenant General Song Yo-ch'an, showed no intention of shooting at demonstrating students. In fact, the army seemed to maintain strict "neutrality" between the Rhee administration and the demonstrators. [33] While the very life of the Rhee administration trembled in the balance, the coercive powers of the regime thus evaporated.

In an attempt to save the Rhee regime with the minimum number of concessions to the demonstrating masses, all the cabinet members submitted resignations after resolving that

Vice-President-elect Yi should immediately renounce the post. Defense Minister Kim Chong-yŏl and Home Minister Hong Chin-gi were sent to persuade Yi to resign. Under the circumstances it took them no time at all to obtain the acquiescence of Yi, whose spirit had already been shaken.[34] His resignation was announced on April 24 with Rhee's approval.

The spontaneous uprising, which originally appeared to have the very limited goals of demanding elimination of some police state measures and the re-election of the Vice-President, transformed itself, in the process of the prolonged and bloody rioting, into a demand to overthrow the entire regime.[35] When some 250 professors of colleges and universities—a revered group of men in Korea—demonstrated on the streets of Seoul on April 25 in support of their students, the uprising definitely became much more than sporadic rioting by youngsters. The citizenry had by now joined the demonstrators in all the major urban centers of South Korea, and they demanded that the entire Rhee regime must go at once. As smiling soldiers freely mingled with crowds, the panic-stricken Presidential entourage became convinced that the army would refuse to fire on any crowd seeking Rhee's resignation.

After a series of conferences in the besieged presidential mansion, President Rhee was finally forced to re-examine his own position. Shortly after 9:30 A.M., April 26, the President asked Defense Minister Kim Chong-yŏl and Martial Law Commander Song Yo-ch'an whether further bloodshed would be avoided if he resigned. Both of them agreed that it would, and the President dictated a statement that he would resign "if the people [so] desire." [36]

By the time American Ambassador McConaughy and United Nations Commander Magruder arrived at the presidential mansion for a 10:30 appointment with the President, the presidential statement had been completed and five representatives of the demonstrating citizenry and students had already been told of the decision by the President himself. When informed of the statement of resignation, Ambassador McConaughy immediately praised Rhee by saying that he was "the George Washington of Korea." No one knows at this time what the American ambassador and the United Nations commander really intended to tell President Rhee when they urgently requested an appointment a few hours before Rhee decided to resign.

In the National Assembly, where nearly two-thirds of the members supposedly belonged to the Liberal Party, a motion demanding Rhee's immediate resignation was passed without debate in the afternoon of April 26. Yi Ki-bung, one of whose sons had been adopted by Rhee, and his entire family committed suicide on April 28 in a cottage on the grounds of the presidential mansion. The adopted son shot them all and killed himself.

The martial law commander, General Song Yo-ch'an, maintained order until the discredited National Assembly hastily convened and appointed on April 27 a caretaker government for a period of three months, to be headed by Hŏ Chŏng (Huh Chung). Since Vice-President Chang had already resigned in protest over the March election, the second-ranking member of the Rhee cabinet was Foreign Minister Hŏ, an American-educated administrator who had served Rhee at different times as a cabinet member, acting premier, and mayor of Seoul. Hŏ had, however, broken with Rhee on sufficient issues to avoid being closely identified with the regime.

On June 15, the Assembly passed an amendment to the Constitution which provided for the Prime Minister to be responsible to the lower house of the national legislature, as executive head of the government. It also changed the office of the President to a largely ceremonial post of Chief of State.

The Assembly then resigned to make way for new national elections.

As to the nature of the situation that led to the overthrow of the Rhee regime, there seem to be many divergent views. Some call the situation that developed between April 19 and April 26 the student "uprising," while others call it the student "revolution." A brief evaluation of the political situation in April, after twelve years of Rhee's administration, may be useful for understanding later developments.

The United Nations Commission for the Unification and Rehabilitation of Korea characterized "the political development" during this period as

the further growth and spread of an active concern on the part of the Korean people for democratic methods and the safeguarding of civil liberties. They have also demonstrated a nation-wide determination to correct abuses of power, root out corruption, and eliminate all possible weaknesses or deficiencies in the political life of the Republic.[37]

One Korean commentator, Min Sŏk-hong, believed that the situation

was certainly a revolution. Moreover, it was a liberal democratic revolution, accomplished by the Koreans themselves. . . .

It would be defined as a revolution; firstly, because it overthrew a dictatorial regime, and secondly, because it unseated a class from its privileged position that was made possible by the Rhee regime.[38]

It was certainly true that the situation resulted in the violent overthrow of the Rhee regime and the privileged establishment around it. To that extent, the change could be termed revolutionary. But whether it originated with such an aim was doubtful. Whether it was a conscious "liberal democratic revolution" accomplished solely by "the Koreans themselves" was again a debatable point. When the youthful students smashed the Liberal Party headquarters and the government newspaper building and when they were being shot at by the police, were they consciously fighting for liberal democracy? Had liberal democratic ideas taken such deep roots in the minds of those young students in the fifteen years since 1945 that they were willing to die for them? It might be comfortable to generalize that they were. Realistic considerations, however, would suggest more negative answers than positive ones. A study conducted in Seoul about two years after the Student Uprising indicated that 86 per cent of a university student body believed that Western democracy was unsuited to Korea at present for various reasons.[39]

Another Korean commentator, Cho Ka-gyŏng, believed that the young students merely provided the "ignition point" that touched off the whole situation.

Though it is generally said that the students were the main body of the revolutionary power, even this statement is open to question; because, in a strict sense, they did not have any distinct, conscious goal of overthrowing or seizing a governmental power. . . . It appeared that the majority of the students might have been quite satisfied with some nullification of the result of the rigged elections and with clean and fair re-elections. The students, therefore, merely provided an ignition point.[40]

Was there then any person or organized group that led the situation toward a political goal in the bloody week in April? Did the opposition party play a significant role? Another Korean observer, Hong I-sŏp, answered negatively.

Who led the April Revolution which was touched off by young students and then joined by the citizenry? The Korean Army merely watched; and the United States played the role of a guardian of students. The Democratic Party, then the opposition group, did precious little except watching the situation that underwent changes minute by minute; and when the governmental authorities were suddenly given up by the Liberals, the Democrats were hardly ready to assume the responsibilities of the government. The demonstrations by professors on April 25 might have played a role in encouraging the citizenry to join the students, but it did not play a leading role. Indeed, the lack of any organized leadership was a significant characteristic of the April Revolution.[41]

How did the students themselves understand their own motives for participating in the demonstration in April? A psychology professor in Seoul made out a set of fourteen hypothetical motives for the student participation in the uprising. He then asked university students in Seoul who participated in the demonstrations to identify their motives for doing so. The result was as follows: [42]

Dissatisfaction with the lawless and corrupt Rhee regime	72%
Anger at police atrocities	65%
Anger at the society ruled by violence	65%
Dissatisfaction with the corrupt society	64%
Dissatisfaction with arrogance of the privileged class	64%
Attempt at supporting organizations defending democracy	53%
Realization that only students can rise up for the nation	48%
Moved by the agitation of newspapers	45%
Anger at distorted reporting by the ruling groups	44%
Anger at the corruption in educational institutions	37%
Anger with the hoodlums who assaulted the students	35%
Inability to sit idly by while other students rose up	17%
Convinced of the success of student uprisings	14%
Moved by the appeals of professors to rise up	13%

Admittedly, the students did not give their own motives in their own words; they were merely identifying themselves with hypothetical motives suggested to them. It is striking, however, that the greatest majority of them thought that they had demonstrated "against" lawlessness, corruption, police brutality and violence, and the arrogant privileged class fostered by the Rhee regime. These were, according to the survey, the five most important motives with which the students identified themselves. Only the sixth reason is "for" the support of "organizations defending democracy." In other words, the most important motives were rather negative ones—opposing the most unsavory developments under the Rhee regime. Only the sixth most important reason was a somewhat indirect but positive one—supporting organizations which defended democracy.

In a similar survey conducted by two Korean political scientists, C. I. Eugene Kim and Kim Ke-soo, a university student body in Seoul listed "Reasons for Student Uprisings" in the following order of importance: "corruption in government," "election riggings," "economic depression," "Rhee in power too long," "police attacking Korea University students," "support of the Vice-President (Chang)," "no specific reasons." [43] Parallels between these two surveys are striking, even to the extent that the first five motives were negative ones and the sixth one was to support the symbol of anti-Rhee forces.

No one would conclude from the above surveys that the situation in April was motivated by negative reasons only or that it completely lacked revolutionary aspects. From the brief examination of the over-all situation in April, however, it appears that the rioting was largely the result of a gigantic, "spontaneous combustion" of resentment against the Rhee regime. The student demonstration was certainly more an uprising than a revolution—to say nothing of a "liberal democratic revolution." It almost completely lacked any conscious, concrete, and positive leadership and programs.

The main physical force that toppled the Rhee regime,

namely the students and citizenry, and the political organization that was to inherit the fruits of the uprising, the Democratic Party, were two different groups. This fact was to prove quite troublesome to the government headed by Democratic Party members and, in fact, fatal to the Second Republic.

Chapter 4

Democracy in the Second Republic

In the minds of many Koreans, the degeneration of the Rhee regime into autocracy was attributable partly to the basic orientation of the original Constitution and the subsequent amendments to it. The views of those who initially favored a responsible cabinet system in 1948 seemed completely vindicated by the failure of a presidential system. The position of those political leaders who had opposed the presidency of Dr. Rhee now seemed justified by concrete and indisputable facts. It was only natural, therefore, that former opposition members, most of whom belonged to the Democratic Party, would now attempt to amend the existing Constitution as a first order of business. Significantly, these Korean leaders perceived at least a part of their pressing political problems in constitutional terms.

Constitutional Amendments

The Constitution of the Second Republic that was established as the consequence of the Student Uprising was a product of full-scale amendments to the fundamental law of President Rhee's First Republic. The amendments were adopted on June 15, 1960, less than two months after the bloody events of April, by a vote of 208 to 3. The Constitution of the Republic of Korea, originally promulgated on July 17, 1948, had thus undergone three major series of amendments in twelve years.[1] The last series of amendments was the most drastic.

Because the 1960 amendments indicate the political and constitutional orientation of the Second Republic, the highlights of these amendments are briefly discussed here. These amendments were mainly aimed at giving substance to the constitutional guarantees of the rights of citizens in Chapter II, abandoning the presidential system in favor of a cabinet system of government, establishing the Central Election Committee and Constitutional Court to give political parties constitutional recognition, and guaranteeing freedom of action.[2]

The first article of the amended Constitution proclaimed that "the Republic of Korea shall be a democratic and republican state," exactly as did the original Constitution. However, because the First Republic could wantonly violate the basic civil liberties, which were enumerated in the Constitution but were subject to subsequent legislation by such phrases as "with the provisions of law," the 1960 amendments eliminated these "escape" phrases. Whereas Article 13 of the original Constitution read that "citizens shall not, except as specified by law, be subject to any restrictions on the freedom of speech, press, assembly, and association," Article 13 of the Second Republic's Constitution deleted the phrase "except as specified by law." Similar "escape" phrases were eliminated from other articles.

The Second Republic's Constitution retained the clause, in Article 28, that "laws imposing restrictions upon the liberties and rights of citizens shall be enacted only when necessary for the maintenance of public order or the welfare of the community," but immediately followed the clause with the warning:

However, such restrictions shall not infringe upon the essential substance of the liberties and rights and no provisions shall be made for license to or censorship on speech and press, nor for the permission for assembly and association.[3]

Article 27 had an added paragraph stating that "the political impartiality and status of public officials shall be guaranteed in accordance with the provisions of law." An addition to Article 75 also called for "ensuring the impartiality of the police." These provisions were added to prevent the recurrence of the phenomenon of public servants becoming political tools of a ruling power, as had been the case in the First Republic.

The most significant amendments were, of course, to provide for a cabinet system of government. Article 51 of the 1960 Constitution stated that the President of the Republic should be simply "the head of the State," while the same article of the First Republic's Constitution had read that the President should be "the head of the Executive Branch of the Government." The President of the Second Republic was to be elected for a five-year term by a two-thirds vote of a joint session of both houses. He was eligible for re-election only once.

The executive power of the Second Republic was vested in a state council headed by the Prime Minister. The State Affairs Council was to be collectively responsible to the House of Representatives. The crucial provision in Article 69 concerning the Prime Minister read:

The Prime Minister shall be nominated by the President and the nomination shall be approved by the House of Representatives.

However, if the President has failed to nominate again within five days from the date of disapproval by the House of Representatives, or when the House of Representatives had disapproved the two consecutive nominations, the Prime Minister shall be elected by the House of Representatives.

Such an approval of election was to require a simple majority of the House members. Article 69 also provided that:

The Prime Minister shall appoint the State Council members and the President shall confirm the appointment.

The Prime Minister and a majority of the State Council members shall be chosen from among members of the National Assembly, except when the House of Representatives has been dissolved.

If the House of Representatives decided upon a vote of nonconfidence in the State (Affairs) Council, it had to resign *en bloc* or dissolve the House of Representatives and call a general election for the members of the House within thirty days after dissolution, according to Articles 35 and 71. A nonconfidence resolution of the House could be passed by a majority vote of the representatives duly elected and seated.

In the First Republic, the President had extensive emergency powers "to issue orders having the effect of law or to take necessary financial dispositions." In the Second Republic, however, the President had the power "to take necessary financial dispositions by the resolution of the State Council," and the Prime Minister was given the power "to issue ordinances having the effect of law." All official acts of the President had to be executed by written documents and all such documents had to be countersigned by the Prime Minister and the cabinet members concerned.

The third major feature of the amendments of 1960 was a

Central Election Committee that was established "for the purpose of conducting fair elections." This nine-member committee was to be composed of three members elected by mutual vote from among the justices of the Supreme Court and six members recommended by political parties.

The provisions for a Constitutional Court comprised the new Chapter VIII. The President of the Republic, the Supreme Court, and the House of Councilors were to designate three judges of the court respectively; and the new chapter stated that "no judge shall be affiliated with any political party nor participate in politics." The Constitutional Court had jurisdiction over the following matters: review of the constitutionality of law; final interpretation of the Constitution; dispute over jurisdiction among state authorities; dissolution of a political party; impeachment trials; and litigation on the election of the President, Chief Justice, and justices of the Supreme Court.

In the First Republic, rights of political parties were presumably protected by the guarantee of freedom of speech, assembly, and association. The Constitution of the Second Republic, however, had a specific provision concerning political parties as an addition to Article 13:

The political parties shall enjoy the protection of the State in accordance with the provisions of law. However, if the purpose or activities of a political party are contrary to the basic democratic rules of the constitution, the Executive shall impeach it with approval of the President, and the Constitutional Court shall decide on the dissolution of such a political party.

According to this provision, therefore, the guarantee of the freedom of action by political parties was an obviously limited one, leaving much to subsequent political developments and the actual applications of the letters of the Constitution.

Political Parties and the Chang Cabinet

After toppling the Rhee regime, the great majority of students promptly left the political world to its habitual denizens and returned to their campuses. The political stage became again crowded with the birth and rebirth of a dozen or more political parties. Some were opportunistic or irresponsible in nature and others sincere in their wish to establish a new political climate, but all were desirous of elbowing their way to power.[4]

Among the parties that sought power during the period of the caretaker government and the national elections of July 29 to establish the Second Republic, the most prominent was the Democratic Party, the only opposition group with any degree of effectiveness during the last years of the Rhee era. The Democrats were plagued, however, by a factional struggle between the Old and New Factions, which had been more or less dormant under adverse conditions during the Rhee period, but was now wide open as the party's chance of occupying the ruling position became virtually certain.[5] Both factions were essentially conservative in nature and, in the area of foreign relations, advocated much the same policy as that pursued by Rhee. An exception was that the Democrats showed a moderate attitude toward Japan. On domestic policy, the Democrats called for an end to corruption, a re-establishment of personal freedoms, and punishment of those responsible for the election frauds under the First Republic.

The Liberal Party rapidly disintegrated now that Rhee was gone. Already in May, observers noted that the only men still identifying themselves as Liberals were those members of the National Assembly whose political labels were too well known.[6] Even within the Assembly, on June 1, 105 out of

138 Liberals publicly and simultaneously broke with the Liberal Party. This left only 33 members with the Liberal affiliation.[7] Subsequently, the Liberal Party evaporated into the thin air of Korean politics. It was evident that party politics had not existed in any real sense.

"Progressive" parties, which had submerged in the Rhee period especially after the execution of Cho Bong-am, were now re-emerging. The Popular Socialist Party was successful in absorbing remnants of the original and outlawed Progressive Party of the late Cho Bong-am, the Democratic Reform Party, and other minor left-wing parties which had become extinct during the Rhee period. The new party demanded a bipartisan approach to foreign relations, while presenting a basically pro-Western line, and advocated "progressive" socio-economic measures. The "progressives" were also split into several warring factions, however, including the group that formed the Korean Socialist Party.[8]

The Korean Independence Party, formerly led by the late Kim Ku and dissolved shortly after the establishment of the Republic, was also revived on June 28, 1960, as a rightist organization. As the election campaigns reached a full swing in July, the Korean political arena was a scene of "unprecedented confusion,"[9] due to the proliferation of political parties.

The outcome of the July 29 elections, however, was that the Democratic Party, both factions taken together, secured 175 seats[10] out of 233 in the lower house. Forty-six seats went to "independent" candidates, and the remainder was shared among four Popular Socialists, two Liberals, one Korean Socialist, and several splinter groups. The fifty-eight members of the House of Councilors were elected as follows: thirty-one Democrats, twenty independents, four Liberals, one Popular Socialist, one Korean Socialist, and one National League of Progressives member.[11]

The Central Election Committee reported that, despite the fact that thousands of voters on off-shore islands could not get to the polls because of stormy weather, 82.6 per cent of the eligible voters cast their ballots. This was the lowest voting percentage in the history of the Republic, but certainly not the lowest compared with the percentages in other countries.

The caretaker government attempted to guarantee an "absolutely free atmosphere for all voters." However, in a land where elections had been repeatedly marred by intimidation, violence, deception, bribery, or outright tampering with ballot boxes, the July 29 elections failed to become suddenly free of these incidents. In many election districts, overly zealous candidates belonging to the New Faction of the Democratic Party and their supporters were guilty of malpractices—much in the pattern of the Liberals in the Rhee era.[12] A result was that winners could not be determined in thirteen election districts until ballotings in these areas were repeated.

The U.N. Commission for the Unification and Rehabilitation of Korea observed the July 29 election with ten teams, each composed of one delegate plus one international and one Korean staff member from the commission secretariat. The chairman of the commission for July, Philippine Ambassador Juan M. Arreglado, said on August 1 that the teams felt that the Korean people had "demonstrated their determination to have free, orderly and fair elections." He was glad that the Central Election Committee had recommended full or partial re-elections in cases where there were "unfavorable or regrettable localized incidents." [13]

In Washington, State Department spokesman Lincoln White said the election appeared to have been "free and honest" despite "isolated incidents" of violence. American Ambassador Walter P. McConaughy noted that the election had "strengthened democracy" in Korea. He also minimized the violence, pointing out that less than 2 per cent of the ballot

boxes were affected. The Ambassador also added that the
embassy teams (reportedly eight) that toured the provinces
found no evidence of official interference, coercion, or other
attempts by the government to influence the vote.[14]

The overwhelming election victory, however, did nothing
to bring together the two factions of the Democratic Party.
In fact, it intensified the factional strife between the Old and
New Factions concerning the question of who should occupy
the presidency, premiership, cabinet posts, and other important positions in the government of the Second Republic. Mr
Yun Po-sŏn of the Old Faction, who was elected on August
12 as the President of the Republic, first named Kim To-yŏn
of his faction as Prime Minister, but the nomination was rejected in the lower house by a 122 to 111 vote. A simple majority of 114 votes was required. President Yun then nominated Chang Myŏn of the New Faction. His nomination was
accepted on August 19 by a vote of 117 to 107 with one ab-
stention—a slim difference of only ten votes and only three
votes more than the absolute minimum required. Already in
the afternoon of August 19, some seventy members of the
Old Faction resolved that they would formally sever their relationship with the Democratic Party and form an opposition
party after absorbing some independents.[15]

As Chang tried to form his cabinet, his real frustrations and
trials began. The "negotiations" between the Old and the
New Factions dragged out. When the composition of the
first Chang cabinet was announced on August 23, a chorus
of disapproval was immediately heard from most directions
because fourteen cabinet-level posts were assigned to eleven
New Faction members, one Old Faction member, and two
independents. It was not until September 12 that Premier
Chang could form a cabinet acceptable to both factions. In
return for the Old Faction's participation in the cabinet,

Premier Chang had to agree that they would be recognized as a "separate" group in the legislature and to guarantee their proportionate share of committee chairmanships and other perquisites.[16] The cabinet announced on September 12 was, for all practical purposes, a "coalition" body of seven New Faction members, five Old Faction members, and two independents.

There had been persistent talk of formally splitting the Democratic Party even during the July election campaign, but many Koreans hoped that the Democrats would somehow remain in a single party to continue to command a working majority in the legislature. With the announcement of the cabinet formation, these Koreans thought that their hope was realized. By the end of September, however, Kim To-yŏn, whose nomination to the premiership had been defeated by the New Faction, had announced that the Democratic Party was irrevocably split and that he was definitely planning to organize a new conservative party.

At the same time, Kim's uncompromising attitude was beginning to alienate some of the other Old Faction members and independents, and after the New Faction officially registered itself under the name of the "Democratic Party," many of the Old Faction members began to make overtures to Premier Chang.[17] At the end of September, Chang's New Faction had only 95 dependable members in the lower house, but by October 19, the total had risen to 118 and, for the first time, Chang appeared to have a parliamentary majority acknowledging his own leadership.

By October 18, 1960, Kim To-yŏn and his supporters finally launched the "New Democratic Party." They offered as a *raison d'être* the necessity of avoiding a one-party dictatorship by the New Faction and the need for an opposition party in the parliamentary system.[18] The fatal split within the

Democrats was thus accomplished, ostensibly in the name of parliamentary democracy.

The factional struggle did not stop there. The so-called "Young Group" of the New Faction had been openly critical of Premier Chang and the "Old Group," obviously because the Chang cabinet did not include youthful members of the Democratic Party.[19] The Young Group members subsequently formed the "New Breeze Society"—with the effect of further dividing the Democratic Party. The internecine, factional warfares of the last period of the Yi Dynasty were repeating themselves in the Second Republic.

Attempting to mollify different factions and groups, Premier Chang reshuffled his cabinet, initially formed on August 23, 1960, three times in less than nine months—on September 12, January 20, and May 3. While the average tenure of ministers under President Rhee was a relatively short period of twenty-two months, it was only six months under Premier Chang. The Home Ministers, who controlled the police force of the country, were most frequently ousted, their average tenure being seven months under the Rhee regime and less than two months in the Chang cabinet.[20] It would have been a miracle had the Chang government been able to function— let alone solve major problems—under these circumstances.

An Avalanche of Problems

With the dramatic and bloody upheaval in Korean politics, the people expected that their daily lives would somehow be improved. After all, many politicians had led them to believe that the root of all the political and economic evils in South Korea was the autocracy of Rhee and the Liberal Party. The annual per capita income in Korea when the Rhee regime was overthrown was only about fifty dollars, one of the lowest in the world.[21] It was, of course, true that ever since the establishment of Liberal Party domination the political climate in Korea had been far from reassuring; society was not one in which economically productive activities were secure, obtaining social recognition and reward. The economic ills of South Korea, however, were not caused solely by the Rhee regime and, by the same token, could not be automatically remedied by the Chang government.

A great majority of the Korean people, however, looked to the Chang government for certain "magic" cures for its desperate economic condition. In response to a request by the Secretariat of the State Affairs Council (cabinet) that they conduct an opinion survey in November, survey groups of eight South Korean universities asked three thousand South Koreans about, among other things, "their most urgent request to the government." The top eight items in the response to the question were as follows: [22]

Relief measures for the unemployed	20.8%
Price stabilization	17.9%
Adjustment of price of farm products	13.8%
Liquidation of usurious loans to farmers and fishermen	11.6%
Crime control and maintenance of order	3.9%
Equitable taxation	3.1%
Support of medium and small business	2.0%
Solution to housing problems	1.0%

Over 70 per cent of the South Koreans surveyed named the solution of economic problems as their "most urgent request to the government."

This fact could have been interpreted in a number of ways, the most obvious one being that the great majority of the Korean people were keenly concerned about economic problems and, therefore, would support the government that would best solve these problems. It was a significant fact that only 3.7 per cent of the same group of respondents unreservedly expressed support for the Chang government, while 51.5 per cent intended to wait and see.[23] These Koreans were, of course, to be utterly disappointed, because the economic ills in the divided and underdeveloped country—in which about two-thirds of the people were engaged in submarginal farming and in which the world's fourth largest standing army was then maintained—were much more deep-seated than most Koreans and the government itself realized.

After the Chang government agreed with the United States that the official exchange ratio between the Korean *hwan* and the American dollar should be "adjusted to correspond to the reality," the exchange ratio of 650 *hwan* to one dollar jumped to 1,300 *hwan* to one dollar. The South Korean economy, which had been dependent on American assistance for a decade and a half, immediately showed the effects of this adjustment. Prices of practically all goods skyrocketed in South Korea, while the purchasing power of the Korean *hwan* abroad declined drastically. Many small and medium businesses collapsed.[24] The unemployment rate in 1960 was about 24 per cent of the available labor force.[25] The battle-cry of the Democrats when they had maintained an opposition to the Rhee regime—"We can't make a living; so let's change!"— could now be turned against their party and the Chang government. The great majority of Koreans had very little to lose economically, no matter what happened to the regime.

Aside from such overwhelming economic problems, the Chang government had to cope with a force that had been little known during the Rhee era. It was the "popular" force unleashed by the Student Uprising. A natural aftermath of such a popular uprising after two generations of suppression was the sudden discovery of "public opinion." [26] The widespread impression since the Student Uprising that anything could be gained by demonstrations now brought people into the streets on every conceivable issue—from bigamy to the new economic agreement with the United States. Estimates placed the number of demonstrations during the one-year period at about 2,000, with over 900,000 participants.[27] With countless unemployed persons idling about, it was not difficult to whip up popular frenzy on any issue.

The unnerving "trend toward a government by demonstrations" was spearheaded by students. For instance, the students invaded the National Assembly on October 11 to demand "revolutionary legislation" imposing stiffer penalties for ousted officials of the Rhee regime. Scores of students wounded during the April uprising physically seized the rostrum of the National Assembly and delivered emotional speeches. Some family members of those who were killed in the April uprising also demonstrated in front of the Assembly, wailing and displaying the pictures of the victims of police brutality and demanding the resignation of assemblymen who hesitated to impose stiffer penalties.

The House of Representatives gave in and another constitutional amendment was hurriedly introduced, adopted, and promulgated. The amendment of November 29, which took the form of a "supplementary rule" to the Constitution, stipulated that the National Assembly

may enact a Special Law to punish the persons who committed unlawful acts in connection with the elections of the President and Vice-President held on March 15, 1960 and the persons who killed or inflicted bodily injury upon, or committed any other unlawful acts against, the citizens protesting to the irregularities; and may enact a Special Law to suspend the citizenship of the persons who committed grave anti-democratic acts taking advantage of their special positions attained before April 26, 1960;

and may enact a Special Law to make the administrative or criminal dispositions of the persons who accumulated properties by unlawful means taking advantage of their positions or powers attained before April 26, 1960. . . .

The Special Law enacted in accordance with the provisions of the preceding two paragraphs may not be amended after their enactment.[28]

The National Assembly of the Second Republic thus empowered itself to enact the most far-reaching *ex post facto* laws, which were to be unamendable once enacted, to dispose of the "traitors to democracy." [29]

Police began re-arresting those who had been released, acquitted of charges relating to election frauds and police brutality. Courts stopped trials then in progress on the basis of laws existing before the promulgation of the constitutional amendment. The sanctity of laws, the legislature, and the courts was swept away by the waves of demonstrations by those who had led the April "revolution."

Finally, on December 31, 1960, a "law concerning the restriction of the civil rights of those who committed anti-democratic acts" [30] was adopted. In the first article, the law declared that it aimed at restricting the "civil rights" of those who performed "notably anti-democratic acts" taking advantage of "special positions" they occupied prior to April 26, 1960. The law then defined the "anti-democratic acts" as those acts that destroyed the "various democratic principles" by violating "the basic rights of the people guaranteed by the Constitution and other laws." The "civil rights" to be restricted by the laws were defined as "the qualification to become a public official" and "the voting right and the right to be elected."

Article 4 listed nine categories of "special positions," the occupants of which were to be automatically regarded as having committed notably anti-democratic acts. The positions covered by the sweeping categories included the Liberal Party's presidential and vice-presidential candidates in the 1960 elections, members of the central committee of the Liberal Party, members of the planning committee of the Central Election Commission of the Liberal Party, cabinet members, secretaries to the President, and secretaries to the Speaker of the House—at the time of the 1960 elections. These so-called "automatic cases" of violators of the law also included any Home Ministry and police officials who could conceivably have had anything to do with the election rigging—from the head of the Security Bureau of the Ministry of Home Affairs down to the heads of local police stations. The mayor and vice-mayor of Seoul Special City and governors of provinces were also "automatic cases." So were the commander and vice-commander of the Taehan Anti-Communist Youth Corps, heads of government-owned enterprises, and important members of the Liberal Party in various localities.[31]

Article 5 of the law listed nineteen different categories of possible violators of the law whose civil rights could be restricted after investigations by an inquiry council. These categories included numerous police detectives, heads of detective sections of police stations, public prosecutors of various ranks, chiefs of staff of the Army, Navy, and Air Force—at the time of the 1960 elections. These so-called "investigatory cases" appeared to cover those who had anything to do with manufacturing "the will of people" to re-elect Rhee and elect Yi Ki-bung.

As to the length of period during which their civil rights would be restricted, the law stipulated that the "automatic cases" would be restricted for seven years and the "investigatory cases" for five.

It should be noted that when this piece of "revolutionary

legislation" was adopted by the House of Representatives on December 31, only six members of the representatives opposed, in a secret ballot, this far-reaching *ex post facto* law, while 161 representatives voted for it.[32] In the high-sounding name of democracy and of revolutionary jurisprudence, these representatives legislated to restrict the constitutionally guaranteed basic civil rights of those who were their political enemies. Legal experts would have difficulties in finding precedents of similar kind and scope.

It would be hard to ascertain whether the legislators simply yielded to pressure from the students to adopt such harsh and anti-democratic legislation or whether the legislators themselves really wished to create conditions in which their own political lives would be prolonged for at least two assembly terms. The students, however, continued to wield their big sticks. In mid-November, 1,500 students, enraged chiefly because their university officials refused to discharge a number of professors who had been Rhee supporters, ransacked the home of the president and chairman of the board of directors of Yŏnse University in Seoul. In a reversal of the brutality that had marked Korean police actions, truckloads of policemen, whose ranks had already been purged since the Student Uprising and whose successors had been intimidated into ineffectiveness, trailed the riotous students but made no attempt to check their violence.

The students' views notwithstanding, much had been accomplished in purging the government and the armed forces of those most guilty of excesses under the Rhee regime. The army was beginning to receive "a long overdue shake-up," and general officers who had grown wealthy under Rhee were facing the choice between court martial and resignation.[33] In early December, the government announced that it had already fired 2,213 men, including 81 police chiefs, in its postelection purge of the National Police.

One of the strangest developments that began in the fall of 1960 was the sudden vocal demand for national unification. The demand appeared to have been initiated by young students, who had not consciously shared the bitter experiences of the Korean War ten years before, and some adult groups began to echo the student demands during the winter and spring of 1960–1961. Many appeared to be acting from sincere nationalistic motives, but soon calls for "neutralist" unification of Korea began to be heard.

Those who feared Communist penetration of the movement could hardly help noticing three things: that it was drawing financial support from leftist elements among Korean residents in Japan, who were in turn backed by the Communist regime in North Korea; that criticism of the United States structured in terms of Communist theory was often incorporated into discussion of unification; and that many of the slogans were surprisingly similar to those used by Radio P'yŏngyang in North Korea and by Communist groups in Japan.[34]

Observers recognized the sincerity of many of the students involved in the unification movement but were disturbed by the mixture of self-confidence and naïveté that characterized many of their statements and actions. Many students actually seemed to feel that they could achieve concrete results by simply meeting with student representatives from North Korea at P'anmunjŏm, where the armistice negotiations had been held to end the Korean War. They seriously talked of marching *en masse* to P'anmunjŏm in a grandiose attempt to hold a unification conference with students from the north.

Yet they seemed unable to realize that in Communist North Korea there could be no free and independent student movements such as theirs in South Korea under the Chang government. Many Koreans failed to agree with the students that the United States, the Soviet Union, and Communist China could effectively guarantee lasting neutrality of Korea. Most surprising, however, was that few students seemed to realize how alarming their activities were to conservative rightist groups and to high-ranking army officers. Naturally, the demonstrations were an extremely serious matter to these groups, particularly to many army officers who might lose their jobs as well as their lives if neutralism should turn out to mean communism.[35] That the North Korean regime enthusiastically welcomed through Radio P'yŏngyang broadcasts the moves made by South Korean students deepened the suspicion of the rightists in South Korea.

In any case, it was true that the great majority of the people, with the exception of the now completely discredited ex-Liberals, enjoyed more freedom under the Chang government than at any other period in Korean history. The open talks by students about marching to P'anmunjŏm to unify the country would have been unthinkable before the Chang period. On the other hand, this sudden, almost unlimited freedom tended to be abused. The young and impatient students repeatedly attempted to dictate their impetuous will to the government. The Prime Minister himself was repeatedly forced to listen to the harangue of the leaders of these students, who were by now called the "fourth branch of the Chang regime."

The abuse of freedom tended to be carried to the extreme by the press. It might be recalled that the amended Constitution of the Second Republic made it impossible for the government to restrict the freedom of the press with the provisions of law. The number of newspapers and periodicals suddenly jumped from about 600 to nearly 1,600 by April, 1961, employing some 160,000 reporters.[36] Few of the new "publications" had printing facilities and some had no fixed place of business. Many of them never printed a single edition; some distributed a few mimeographed sheets only. Their principal business, and in some instances their only business, was blackmail. Furthermore, it was an open secret that money was flowing into some of these publications from the leftist elements among Korean residents in Japan,[37] who took advantage of the somewhat improved relations between Korea and Japan under the Chang government.

Some strong voices were raised to urge the Chang government that these excessive enjoyments of "freedom" must be firmly curbed before they really got out of hand. Premier Chang himself, however, declared in his answer to a representative's query that the virtual "impotence" of the police meant that the Korean people now "enjoyed all the rights and freedom guaranteed by the Constitution." [38] Both the Premier and the representatives, however, appeared to ignore the fact that organized gangsters and hoodlums, by taking advantage of that "impotence," made life insecure in many urban centers.

In the "free atmosphere" of the Chang government, corruption at every level became increasingly evident as did the practices of nepotism, now that all the Liberal elements were to be removed from every layer of central and local government. Meanwhile, business and industry stagnated, since many successful businessmen were now accused of having illicitly amassed fortunes in the Rhee period. Millions of unemployed were still without relief. The farmers were desperate—caught between crop failures and usurious interest rates on loans, often as high as 80 per cent per year. The people began to wonder whether Prime Minister Chang was "the most tender-hearted gentleman or the most ignorant bystander." [39]

Premier Chang was not an ignorant bystander; he had had his hands full to keep his "coalition" cabinet from disintegrating ever since the Old Faction of the Democratic Party had openly broken away to form the New Democratic Party. With a precarious majority supporting the cabinet in the

House of Representatives, the Chang government had difficulties for months on end in getting even the budget bill for 1961 passed.

As early as the first part of December, 1960, the New Democrats in the House of Representatives were boisterously demanding the resignation of the Chang cabinet *en bloc* or the dissolution of the "impossible" Assembly, which now did not provide a comfortable majority to any group.[40] But the last general elections had been held scarcely more than four months before. The only way out for Premier Chang was frequent reshuffles of his cabinet members in agonizing attempts to meet the demands of different factions in the Assembly as well as within his Democratic Party, which was now divided between the younger and older groups— certainly an exasperating state of affairs. The bickering and virulent attacks and counterattacks among all these different factions continued throughout the existence of the regime.

While the maddening game of musical chairs was being played in and around the Chang cabinet, the Korean people as a whole tended to become more confused and exasperated with politics and politicians than ever before. They had already experienced five general Assembly elections and three elections for the presidency and vice-presidency. They had read about or experienced the 1952 political crisis in Pusan and another political crisis in 1954 again relating to a constitutional amendment. Above all, the Student Uprising had violently overthrown a hated regime and the Liberal Party. The ruling groups had changed, but the overall situation had not improved much.

In the elections for mayor of Seoul and governors of the nine provinces of South Korea held on December 29, 1960, an average of only 38.2 per cent of the qualified voters actually cast their ballots.[41] This was an astonishing drop in voter participation. Again, in a by-election from the Mapo district in Seoul held on February 10, 1961, ballots were cast by only about 40,000 citizens out of 110,000 qualified voters and 210,000 residents of the district. The participation here was also about 38 per cent, the lowest since the establishment of the Republic of Korea in 1948.

These facts were probably indications that the Korean people were rapidly losing interest in elections and in important political questions of the day, possibly because political changes had failed to improve their own lives and had merely resulted in further confusion and exasperation. The people were plainly lethargic and apathetic.[42] Despite vague rumors of another political crisis,[43] South Korea remained generally calm on the surface—until the early dawn of May 16, 1961, less than nine months after the formation of the first Chang cabinet, when some elements of the army swiftly executed a *coup d'état*.

PART II

REORIENTATION
AFTER THE COUP

Chapter 5

The 1961 *Coup d'Etat*

Speculations on the possibility of a military *coup d'état* in Korea had been heard ever since the "political crisis" of May–July, 1952, when President Rhee had declared martial law in the wartime capital area of Pusan to ensure the passage of the first series of constitutional amendments. It had been fairly common knowledge that at the outset of the "political crisis" President Rhee had summoned General Yi Chong-ch'an, then Army Chief of Staff, to Pusan and ordered that a division of army troops be immediately made available to the Martial Law Command. General Yi politely but firmly declined to do so, on the ground that every soldier was needed at the battle line. This was the first known incident of an army general disobeying a command of the constitutional commander-in-chief of the Korean armed forces.

As this incident was related by word of mouth among the officer corps of Korean Army headquarters in Taegu, there were whispers of "doing away with the people around the President," or possibly the President himself, if he insisted on utilizing a large number of troops for his own political battles. The United Nations Command was known to have expressed, through General James A. Van Fleet, its extreme displeasure at the President's demands, and the matter was never brought to a public confrontation. Nevertheless, the incident and the thoughts that crossed the minds of some Korean army officers were probably not completely erased by later events.[1]

As the Korean War progressed, the military forces were rapidly strengthened, becoming the fourth largest armed force in the world in terms of sheer numbers. Its million mark was surpassed only by the armies of Communist China, the Soviet Union, and the United States. Even after the Korean armistice, its strength could not be drastically reduced because the military situation in the Far East, and in the divided country itself, necessitated a huge standing army in South Korea. In postwar Korea, the armed forces remained the most powerful and effective organization in the nation, in both the absolute and the relative senses. By contrast, most other organizations in the nation were embryonic, parasitic, or anemic. In the name of the defense of freedom, South Korea had become an immense garrison.

Forces Leading to the Coup

At the end of the war, the huge standing army suddenly faced a prolonged period of relative inactivity. The officer corps of the Korean Army was freed from the grueling daily challenges of the war. Numerous officers and men were married in the months following the armistice and began to know the warmth as well as the financial responsibilities of being family men. Many young officers also managed to continue their college education that had been interrupted by the war, while others began receiving advanced military training both in Korea and in the United States.

Political and economic problems gradually loomed larger in the minds of many officers. High-ranking government officials, along with those businessmen who had established intricate connections with the powerful top layer of the Liberal Party and many of the generals of the armed forces, enjoyed a luxurious life in postwar Korea—partly thanks to American economic assistance or the misuse of it. But the great majority of field- and company-rank officers and enlisted men of the military forces led a life at the subsistence level, while innumerable families which had lost their breadwinners, many of them soldiers, were on the verge of starvation.

Political disorder in Korea, particularly the repeated and brazen election-rigging under the Liberal Party, had a direct effect on the armed forces. Many of the top-ranking generals were directly involved in delivering the hundreds of thousands of votes from the armed service personnel to Rhee and his supporters. Numerous generals and admirals no longer commanded the respect of their officers and men, who knew all too well how corrupt and cowardly their superiors had become in order to retain their positions as commanders of large armed units. President Rhee, Yi Ki-bung, and, toward the end of the Rhee era, even some powerful secretaries of these men knew how to keep the generals in place by carefully timed and screened promotions, forced retirements, and the consignment of some of the more ambitious ones to honorific diplomatic assignments abroad.[2]

The gradual disintegration of military discipline from the top down coincided with a series of developments abroad that stirred the imaginations of the numerous young officers who were rapidly becoming politically conscious. These external developments included the uprisings in Egypt led by the Society of Free Officers, culminating in the assumption of the Egyptian presidency in 1956 by Colonel Gamal Abdel Nasser, the emergence of General Ne Win as the strongman of Burma in 1958, and the seizure of political power by General Ayub Khan of Pakistan in 1958.

Already in February, 1960, while President Rhee and his Liberal Party were preoccupied with ensuring victory at any cost in the scheduled March 15 elections, a military *coup d'état* was being planned. The mastermind of the plan was Major General Chung Hee Park, then logistics base commander in Pusan.[3] Participants in the planning at this stage included Major General Yi Chu-il, chief of staff of the Second Army; Major General Kim Tong-ha, commander of the Marine Division at P'ohang; Lieutenant Colonel Kim Chongch'ŏl, commander of the 33rd Antiaircraft Artillery Battalion stationed in Pusan; and Lieutenant Colonel Kim Chong-p'il of the Army Headquarters G-2 (intelligence).[4] They decided to stage the coup on May 8, 1960, since Army Chief of Staff Song Yo-ch'an was slated to leave for the United States on May 5. They hoped to mobilize some 5,000 soldiers to execute the coup, mostly from the Logistics Command, the Marine Division in P'ohang, the 36th Army Division in Andong, and antiaircraft artillery battalions.

Then came the Student Uprising of April 19, 1960, that cracked the thin veneer of order covering the nation's profound socio-economic and political disarray. Characteristically, President Rhee declared martial law, but the army under the martial law commander, Lieutenant General Song Yoch'an, evidently decided not to block the demonstrating students and citizenry, as some policemen attempted. At the most critical juncture, when the very survival of the Rhee regime was at stake, the army command's political decision to be "neutral" in the situation was undoubtedly one of the most decisive forces which pursuaded Rhee to step down. The significance of this inaction by the military in bringing about the ouster of the Rhee regime was not lost on the officer corps, and this realization was but a step removed from a conviction that an action by the military would definitely produce spectacular results.

With the "resignation" of Rhee, hopeless divisions among themselves rendered the civilian politicians, who had to fill the political vacuum created by the upheaval, bewildered and incapable of filling that vacuum or of governing the nation in turmoil. Conditions were already ripe in 1960 for the armed forces to intervene in the political sphere. The time shortly after the Student Uprising, however, was not propitious for the military to take drastic political action, for the majority of the Korean people had great expectations that political and economic conditions were going to improve rapidly under the new regime of the Democrats. The military group that had planned a coup for May, 1960, now decided to wait and see.

As numerous members of the Rhee regime and of the Liberal Party were being driven out of their positions of power and influence in every sphere of activity in South Korea, it was only natural that there should arise a demand within the armed forces for the elimination of those top-ranking officers who were either closely identified with the fallen Rhee regime or who were reputed to be "incompetent and corrupt" in their commanding positions. It was also natural that the most effective demands for the "purification" of the top level of the military establishment should come from the upper-middle layer of the military hierarchy, namely, lieutenant colonels and colonels.

These officers were sandwiched between the generals, who enjoyed numerous and substantial privileges, and company-rank officers, the workhorses of the officer corps, who had to be largely preoccupied with their daily chores. The colonels occupied important positions in the chain of command of the army, as battalion commanders or general staff members of various units, from Army headquarters down to combat units. In their positions, they had direct control over field-rank officers and frequent contact with many generals who were targets of their daily criticism. They had long felt a sense of uncertainty about their future. The top layer of the armed service had been overcrowded by generals; the field-rank officers could hardly hope to enter any other profession, even if they wished to leave the military career, since most of them had little or no skill that could secure satisfactory employment in a country where over 20 per cent of the work force was unemployed.

It was a group of lieutenant colonels—specifically, members of the "eighth graduating class," [5] or the class of 1949, of the Korean Military Academy—that initially formulated five measures for "military purification" on May 8, 1960. These measures were:

1. Punishment of top military officers who collaborated with the Liberals in rigging the 1960 presidential elections.
2. Punishment of military officers who amassed wealth illegally.
3. Elimination of incompetent and corrupt commanders.
4. Political neutrality of the armed forces and elimination of factionalism.
5. Improvement of treatment for military servicemen.[6]

Eight members of the "eighth graduating class" resolved to recommend these measures to General Song Yo-ch'an. But the plan fizzled. The Chief of Staff learned of the scheme even before the recommendation was submitted to him in the name of the lieutenant colonels, and he decided to detain six of them. General Song himself, who had been Army Chief of Staff from the last year of the Rhee regime, had been generally blamed for collaborating with the Liberal Party in rigging the 1960 elections among the army troops.

The six lieutenant colonels were quietly released after two days of heated discussions at Army headquarters about charging them with plotting rebellion—a serious offense indeed, if convicted. General Song himself resigned from his post on

May 20, 1960, and subsequently retired from active military service, ostensibly assuming all responsibility for settling this unrest in the army and also for quelling other rumblings. Arrangements had already been made for General Song to leave the country temporarily to attend George Washington University in Washington, D.C., as a "special student."

What was significant in this development was not that General Song had resigned, since his resignation was expected sooner or later in view of his involvement as Army Chief of Staff in the election rigging, but the fact that it came at that particular time. As the "Young Turks" grumbled, General Song, or "Tiger Song," appeared to whimper instead of roar. The general who personified, in his capacity as Army Chief of Staff, the top-level establishment of the military was squeezed out of his position and of active military service. The "military purification movement" had an auspicious start and began to gather momentum.

Immediately after the establishment of the Second Republic in August, 1960, eleven lieutenant colonels [7] decided to call on Defense Minister Hyŏn Sŏk-ho of the Chang cabinet to urge "purification" of the military. Minister Hyŏn decided not even to receive them, and the young officers were taken to the provost marshal's office and severely reprimanded for their conduct. It was in the evening of the very same day that nine indignant colonels met with Major General Chung Hee Park at a Seoul restaurant and unanimously resolved to execute a coup. Every one of them readily agreed on the futility of reform efforts through peaceful recommendations. They agreed that drastic reforms were urgently needed in the entire political and governmental establishment.

What had begun as a limited "military purification" movement aimed at dislodging from the military hierarchy some "corrupt and inefficient" generals had now acquired the revolutionary objective of overthrowing the Second Republic and everything that was symbolized by it. What should be noted is that the younger colonels, mostly of the "eighth graduating class," including Lieutenant Colonel Kim Chong-p'il, General Park's nephew-by-marriage, joined hands with the force led by General Park, who had originally planned a coup for May, 1960. The nucleus of a revolutionary movement was born.

On September 24, a group of sixteen officers confronted Lieutenant General Ch'oe Yŏng-hi, who had succeeded General Song as Army Chief of Staff, with a demand to resign. These officers were referred to an army court martial on charges of disrupting military discipline. After prolonged trials on which the attention of the entire officer corps was focused, only one colonel was sentenced, on December 12, to three months' imprisonment. Subsequently, however, Lieutenant Colonels Kim Chong-p'il and Sŏk Chŏng-sŏn, both of the "eighth graduating class," were put on reserve status.[8] It meant to them that their military career had come to an abrupt end and that they were thrown into a sea of the unemployed. It also meant that the revolutionary movement had now definitely reached a point of no return for them, and that the movement gained at least two full-time workers.

The officers met with increasing frequency to plot the coup. From late 1960 to early 1961, the coup organization network expanded to officers of the First Army, various military units stationed in the Seoul area, military district commands, and many reserve divisions. The Marine Corps, which had conceived its own plan to stage a coup, joined the army officers, largely due to the efforts of Major General Kim Tong-ha and Brigadier General Kim Yun-gŭn. By the first part of April, 1961, organization of the coup forces was completed.[9]

What was astonishing was the fact that an organization involving at least "250 officers of all ranks"[10] could be kept a secret—or an open secret—for several months. It either demonstrated almost superhuman mastery by all these officers of the intricate art of clandestine, subterranean activities, or the inability or unwillingness of the top-level commanders of the Korean military to command and supervise their officers. It also showed the fundamental lack of loyalty of all these officers, probably including the top-level generals, to the civilian government that constitutionally commanded the military. Numerous subsequent pronouncements to the contrary notwithstanding, it furthermore demonstrated the fundamental lack of a commitment by these officers to the political system that was symbolized by the government of the Second Republic.

The Blitz

The coup forces struck the heart of the Second Republic, Seoul, in the chilly pre-dawn hours of May 16, 1961. The only physical force needed to topple the Democratic regime was about 1,600 men.[11] Although the Army Chief of Staff, Lieutenant General Chang To-yŏng, who was reputed to have been hand-picked for the post by Premier Chang himself, allegedly knew for many hours about the final timetable of the coup forces,[12] the total military strength that was actually mobilized in an attempt to block the revolutionary troops at the Han River bridge was only about fifty military policemen. Only a handful of these military policemen was wounded, as the coup forces quickly overpowered the half-hearted and feeble opposition. This was the extent of the armed resistance mustered up in its defense by the government of the Second Republic, which supposedly commanded one of the world's largest standing armies.

The Chief of Staff allegedly learned about the final plans

of the coup group shortly before 11 P.M., May 15. The Marine Corps spearhead of the revolutionary forces reached the south end of the Han River bridge at 3:20 A.M., May 16. Chief of Staff Chang telephoned Prime Minister Chang at about 3:30 A.M. to inform him of the shootings at the Han River. At 4:10 A.M., the Chief of Staff again called the Prime Minister, this time urging him to escape from his residence immediately. Premier Chang and his wife, accompanied by a lone bodyguard, a police sergeant, had the driver of his black jeep head for the residential compound of American Embassy personnel. While the guards of the compound sought permission from their superior to open the main gate, reporters of the *Hanguk Ilbo*, across the street from the compound, rushed out to ascertain the identity of those who were seeking admittance to the American compound at that early hour. Chang then ordered his driver to head for another destination —the Carmelite convent in northeastern Seoul.[13]

For two eventful days, the world outside the Carmelite nunnery knew little about the whereabouts of the Premier of the Second Republic. According to his bodyguard, Chang saw only a "foreign priest" and Donald Whittaker, one of his American consultants, while in hiding. The bodyguard also placed a telephone call to the American Embassy on the Premier's behalf on the morning of the coup.[14]

Citizens of Seoul woke up to hear a broadcast over the Seoul Central Radio Station that the Second Republic was overthrown and that "the military authorities" had taken over "the executive, legislative, and judicial branches of the state" and organized a "Military Revolutionary Committee" consisting of five generals. The citizenry then saw that tanks and soldiers in full combat gear were posted at strategic positions in Seoul. An emergency martial law was declared, along with a 7 P.M. to 5 A.M. curfew. The first three decrees of the

Military Revolutionary Committee froze all bank assets, closed airports and harbors, placed publications under strict censorship, and forbade assembly—under pain of severe punishment.[15] "Speechless citizens . . . just watched" the fully armed soldiers in action.[16]

Six "revolutionary pledges" were repeatedly broadcast throughout the day. They were:

1. Positive, uncompromising opposition to Communism is the basis of our policy.

2. We shall respect and observe the United Nations Charter, and strengthen our relations with the United States and other Free World nations.

3. We shall eliminate corruption, and eradicate other social evils which had become prevalent in our country; we shall inculcate fresh and wholesome moral and mental attitudes among the people.

4. We shall provide relief for poverty-stricken and hungry people, and devote our entire energies toward the development of a self-sustaining economy.

5. We shall strengthen our material power and determination to combat Communism, looking forward to the eventual achievement of our unchangeable goal of national unification.

6. As soldiers, after we have completed our mission, we shall restore the government to honest and conscientious civilians, and return to our proper military duties. As citizens, we shall devote ourselves without reservation to the accomplishment of these tasks, and to the construction of a solid foundation for a new and truly democratic republic.[17]

Decree No. 4, issued in the afternoon of May 16, proclaimed that the Military Revolutionary Committee "took over the entire Chang regime"; that the House of Representatives, the House of Councilors, and provincial councils throughout South Korea were immediately dissolved; that all political and social activities were banned; that cabinet ministers and vice-ministers were to be arrested; that the Military Revolutionary Committee was to take over all state organizations; and that the use of violence would be severely punished.

While the gigantic dragnet was out for members of the Chang cabinet, President Yun Po-sŏn remained conspicuously exempt from the military operations to oust "the present corrupt and incompetent government and politicians." President Yun, the constitutional head of the state and standard-bearer of the Old Faction Democrats, still occupied the Blue House, the presidential mansion. In fact, Major General Chung Hee Park himself paid Yun a visit in the early morning of May 16 to seek his support for the coup and presidential sanction for martial law. As General Park was emphasizing the necessity of the revolution and reported on its success to that moment, Yun reportedly stated: "I had believed revolution inevitable." [18] While refusing to sanction the martial law already declared, President Yun agreed to write personal letters to all Army Corps commanders urging them to help resolve the national crisis without bloodshed. At that early phase of the revolt, when only a few thousand troops were actually guarding the Military Revolutionary Committee and when it was widely feared that certain front-line units including the powerful First Army might launch a countercoup attack, the President's move was significant. Later that day two teams of personal secretaries to the President aboard military planes provided by the Military Revolutionary Committee carried the presidential message to Army Corps commanders.[19]

When General Park returned to army headquarters following the meeting with President Yun, he received a report that Lieutenant General Yi Han-lim, First Corps commander, had ordered the mobilization of at least three divisions under Yi's command as a counterrevolutionary move.[20] General Park immediately ordered the establishment of a Seoul area defense command, consisting of the few thousand revolutionary forces in Seoul and all available military police companies. A blood bath within the South Korean Army appeared a distinct possibility.

This possibility was increased by the activities of the highest-ranking Americans in Korea. The United Nations Commander, U.S. General Carter B. Magruder, learned in the pre-dawn hours of the military take-over from the Korean Army Chief of Staff, who telephoned to inform him of the rapid-moving developments. Magruder asked Chang To-yŏng about the "real character" of the revolutionary forces. Chang replied: "I don't know whether it's a mutiny or revolution." [21] Thus, the Korean Army Chief of Staff professed not to know whether the military action constituted an action by a small number of dissidents or a large-scale effort to overthrow the Second Republic.

By 6 A.M., General Magruder and Minister Marshall Green, the American chargé d'affaires, were busily attempting to evaluate the situation. The picture was far from clear, and they decided that they had to see Prime Minister Chang. The American Embassy tried everything to locate the Prime Minister, who was rumored to have taken refuge with the Embassy, a U.S. military base, or a foreign diplomatic mission. The Prime Minister was not to be found.

One point, however, was immediately clear: that the movement of Korean troops without the consent of the United Nation's Commander had transgressed the U.N. Commander's authority, arising from the 1950 Taejŏn Agreement, to exercise sole operational control over the South Korean armed forces. After long deliberations during which political aspects of the upheaval obviously received keen attention, the American military commander and the ranking diplomatic repre-

sentative reached an important decision to initiate a move
aimed at restoring the *status quo ante* in South Korea. They
agreed on issuing separate statements immediately, before the
10:30 deadline of afternoon dailies in Seoul—although no
advice had yet been received from Washington. Magruder's
statement read:

> General Magruder, in his capacity as Commander-in-Chief of
> the United Nations Command, calls upon all military personnel
> in his command to support the duly recognized Government of
> the Republic of Korea headed by Prime Minister Chang Myun.
> General Magruder expects that the chiefs of Korean Armed
> Forces will use their authority and influence to see that control is
> immediately returned back to governmental authorities and that
> order is restored in the armed forces.

Green stated:

> The position taken by the Commander-in-Chief of the United
> Nations Command in supporting the freely elected and con-
> stitutionally established Government of the Republic of Korea
> is one in which I fully concur.
> I wish to make it emphatically clear that the United States
> supports the constitutional Government of the Republic of Korea
> as elected by the People of the Republic last July and as con-
> stituted by election last August of the Prime Minister.

Thus the two top-ranking Americans chose to make it
clear that the U.S. representatives on the spot supported the
democratic government headed by Premier Chang. The tone
of the statements unmistakably reflected both their conviction
that the "freely elected" Chang government had to be restored and their expectation that the bulk of the Korean
armed forces would remain loyal to the "constitutionally established" government and actively subjugate the revolutionary troops. The American military commander, with the full

and public support of America's chief diplomat in Korea, was in fact urging that the Korean armed forces follow his command, both political and military. The full authority and prestige of the United States were emphatically invoked. These statements were the only ones to be heard in defense of a "freely elected" or democratic government in South Korea in the wake of the military coup.

The statements were rushed to Seoul newspapers by messengers, and another set was sent to the American-controlled Voice of the United Nations Command. Although the Voice at once began broadcasting the statements, Korean newspapers were already under strict censorship by the coup forces. Stories on the statements were literally "blacked out," and their impact on Koreans was largely lost.

President Yun, having heard the Voice broadcast of the Magruder-Green statements, urgently summoned the two Americans to the presidential mansion. The Americans lost no time in demanding presidential sanction to launch a counter-revolution. Magruder wished to order the mobilization of 40,000 men—many times the strength of the revolutionaries holding the Seoul area at the time, he said—to encircle the capital and force the revolutionaries to return to their posts. The American general asked Yun, as chief of state and commander-in-chief of the Korean armed forces, to agree to this plan. Magruder now estimated—shortly after 11 A.M.—the revolutionary strength in the Seoul area at 3,500 men, almost precisely correct.[22]

The American general told Yun that the powerful and mobile First Army to the north was almost entirely opposed to the coup and that there was also anti-coup strength in southern locations. Lieutenant General Yi Han-lim, commander of the First Army, had urged his troops to maintain "strict neutrality" from revolutionary moves.

Minister Green then emphasized that the coup was unconstitutional and declared flatly that the United States could not
support it. If the coup succeeded, the American minister predicted, there would be a second and a third coup—all of
which would thwart the development of democracy in Korea.
Green fully endorsed the American commander's request for
the President's agreement to counterrevolutionary action.
Korea stood at a brink of civil war. On President Yun depended whether or not the Korean armed forces would be
split into two warring camps.

Yun resolved that South Korea could hardly afford such a
peril, particularly in view of the ever-present menace from the
Communist army poised in North Korea. No, Yun declared
to Magruder and Green, he could not agree to a mobilization
of the Korean armed forces to crush the coup. The President
of the Second Republic, who was merely a ceremonial head of
state with the Chang cabinet, also observed that a military
revolution, though not desirable, was perhaps inevitable, since
the Chang Myŏn government had lost the people's confidence.

While each passing minute was affecting the future of
Korea, Yun invited both Magruder and Green to lunch.
Green, the diplomat, agreed. Magruder, the soldier, excused
himself, explaining that he was too busy. He called an emergency staff meeting at his headquarters and decided that the
coup forces had to be crushed, since "the coup was an illegal
action taken by a small group of soldiers and did not reflect
the will of the Korean people." [23] He decided that units of the
Korean First Army and of the U.S. armored division had to be
immediately mobilized, and so instructed Lieutenant General
Yi Han-lim and General John L. Ryan, commander of the
First U.S. Corps. General Magruder subsequently visited with
General Yi at the latter's headquarters for a strategy session
of nearly an hour.

The First Army had already been paralyzed for any counterrevolutionary moves, however, due to effective infiltration of the general and special staffs by determined prorevolutionary officers. Every move General Yi made was immediately reported to the Military Revolutionary Committee in Seoul, and this fact, too, was made known to Yi, who was virtually a prisoner in his own command post. Menacingly armed colonels and lieutenant colonels threatened to "arrest" the Commander or to "dispose of him." It was becoming increasingly clear to General Yi that any order to march against the revolutionary forces in Seoul would be violently rejected by numerous officers and men of his field army.

General Yi probably saw the handwriting on the wall. He would not be allowed to become a heroic defender of democracy and constitutionally established government alongside the Americans.[24] Some three hours after the visit by General Magruder to the First Army headquarters, a public statement in the name of General Yi was issued simultaneously by General Yi's headquarters and by the military junta in Seoul stating that General Yi supported the revolution "together with all of the officers and men under his command."[25] This statement, issued at about 7 P.M., May 17, clinched the success of the military takeover.

With this announcement, anti-coup strength dissipated. If any forces were to crush the revolutionary movement, they now had to be American troops. Such an action was unthinkable to the United States, although the Washington envoy of the defunct Chang government heatedly demanded that the United Nations Command immediately "restore its control over the Korean armed forces."[26]

For nearly two days after the coup, the U.S. State and Defense departments refused to comment on the Korean situation on the ground that it was in a "fluid" condition. As hopes of reversing the military coup collapsed, State Department officials were reported to be "concentrating on trying to salvage some vestige of democratic rule in Korea."²⁷ Under Secretary of State Chester Bowles was now reported to have said that the coup leaders were mainly interested in cleaning up corruption and not in setting up a permanent military dictatorship. Obviously, Washington was attempting to adjust itself to the *fait accompli* in Korea.

It was in the morning of May 18 that Premier Chang, after two days of hiding, contacted General Chang To-yŏng through Donald Whittaker. Escorted by Chang and Whittaker, pale-faced Premier Chang was driven to the capitol to preside over the last cabinet meeting of the nine-month-old Democratic administration. The meeting, which was attended by nine members of the thirteen-man cabinet, decided on an *en masse* resignation of the cabinet to clear the stage for a new ruling body. When the final cabinet session was over shortly after noon, May 18, the Second Republic of Korea was formally declared dead.

Throughout these developments, some members of the Military Revolutionary Committee had felt nagging apprehension about the attitude of Washington toward a military regime in South Korea. After all, South Korea had been heavily dependent on United States assistance, both economic and military. Washington did not disassociate itself from the Magruder-Green statements of May 16 which urged the revival of the Democratic administration. In an extraordinary move, the chairman of the Military Revolutionary Committee, Lieutenant General Chang To-yŏng, sent a special message on May 18 to President John F. Kennedy expressing the committee's desire to maintain "the most friendly ties" with the United States. The uncustomary message stated, in part:

On behalf of the Military Revolutionary Committee I wish to express my sincere respect and gratitude to the Government and people of your country for the assistance and contribution made toward the progress and prosperity of the Republic of Korea. It is the aim of the Republic of Korea *to uphold democracy, based on liberty, equality* and good neighborliness.

Although the April revolution of 1960 carried out by students was successful with the overwhelming support of the Korean people and international sympathy, after one year since the assumption of power by the Democratic Party the people still find themselves in the condition of starvation and despair, and the Government continued to follow the ill practices and corruption of the past. This situation has resulted in endangering our capacity to combat effectively the Communist threats.

Unable to let the situation deteriorate any further, at dawn on May 16, 1961, the military acted to overthrow the Government and took complete control of the executive, legislative and judiciary powers of government. Thus, we embarked upon the sacred revolutionary task of overthrowing the corrupt and inefficient regime and of saving the people and the country.[28]

The message—which read more like a hastily written and translated plea or apology—then summed up the first five of the six revolutionary pledges that had been announced on the morning of the coup. It then continued:

Finally, at any time upon completion of our mission we will hand over the control of the Government to clean and conscientious civilians and to [*sic*] return to our proper duties of the military.

Please rest assured, Excellency, of the integrity of the Committee, and we sincerely hope that the most friendly ties existing between our two countries will continue to be strengthened.

On May 19, the official State Department spokesman, Lincoln White, read a statement "understood to have been cleared by President Kennedy." [29] The terse statement, the first one to be formally issued by the Department of State on the fourth day after the coup, read:

It has been our purpose in Korea to help the Korean people achieve, *through democratic processes,* stability, order, constitutional government and the rule of law as the essential basis for sound economic growth and improvement in the welfare of the people as well as for the defense of the country against any possible communist threat.

This continues to be our purpose.

We are encouraged by the strong intent of the military leaders in Korea to return the government to civilian hands.[30]

A formal response of a sort to General Chang's message to President Kennedy was made more than a week later, not in the name of the President, but by Minister Green, and not to General Chang. The statement was addressed to Kim Hong-il, who had become Korean Foreign Minister under the military junta. Minister Green acknowledged the May 18 message to President Kennedy and stated that his government "noted with approval the pledges set forth in General Chang's message." The American minister then singled out a pledge, as had the State Department spokesman: that the United States government "notes with satisfaction the expression of intention to return the Government to civilian control." [31] Green then reminded Kim that the United States had endeavored to assist the government and people of Korea in their efforts to "maintain freedom through democratic progress." The message concluded: "My Government trusts that the traditional friendly relations between our two countries will continue and that we shall together continue our cooperation in promoting the well-being and strength of Korea." [32]

Despite the obvious diplomatic cold shoulder given to the Chairman of the Military Revolutionary Committee by the

United States, this message was a relief to the committee, since the United States government had evidently decided to accept the revolutionary pledges at their face value and had adopted an attitude of wait-and-see, instead of active opposition. It should be noted that General Chang's message emphasized that the national goal of Korea still was "to uphold democracy" and that both the State Department statement and the American minister's message reminded the Koreans that the United States aim in Korea was to help Koreans uphold democracy and that the United States expected the restoration of a civilian government. In any case, the possibility of United States intervention, which the Military Revolutionary Committee had feared, was gone. The military takeover was now truly a *fait accompli*.

Chapter 6

Rule by the Military Junta

As the military takeover became a firmly established fact, the Military Revolutionary Committee was renamed the Supreme Council for National Reconstruction (SCNR). It was announced that the Council now was the nation's "supreme governing organ," with both executive and legislative powers, plus administrative control over the judiciary.

President Yun Po-sŏn, one of the most puzzling figures in the events after the coup, announced in a brief public statement his intention to resign as head of state, but was immediately persuaded by the military authorities to reverse his decision. His initial statement was issued on May 19, and the reversal came on the following day. Since foreign diplomats were accredited to him as the President, his decision to retain the otherwise meaningless presidency precluded a diplomatic crisis that the new military government might have encountered had he vacated the only remaining constitutional office of the Second Republic. With Yun remaining as president, there was little technical need for formal recognition of the new government.

The Transformation

Although the announcement that the Supreme Council was the "supreme governing organ" of the nation came on May 19, the Law Regarding Extraordinary Measures for National Reconstruction, which defined the functions and powers of the Council, was promulgated on June 6.[1] The political dynamics of post-coup Korea were most dramatically reflected in the rapid centralization of power in the Supreme Council. This relatively brief law superseded the Constitution simply by having Article 24, the last article, declare that those provisions of the Constitution that might conflict with the law regarding extraordinary measures "shall be governed by this Law." The basic rights of the citizens, so painstakingly guaranteed in numerous provisions of the Constitution, were now contracted drastically, according to Article 3, "to such extent as is not inconsistent with the fulfillment of the tasks of the Revolution." The General Provisions of the law, however, declared: "The Supreme Council for National Reconstruction shall be established as an extraordinary measure intended for the *reconstruction of the Republic of Korea as a genuine democratic republic*" (italics mine).

The Council was to be a compact, tightly regimented, and powerful nucleus of the revolutionary government. The number of the supreme councilors was to be neither more than thirty-two nor less than twenty. According to Article 4, they were to be elected from among military officers on active duty "who are deeply imbued with the cause of the May 16 Military Revolution." The tightly knit character of the Council was to be guaranteed by the provision that additional councilors should be elected by the supreme councilors duly seated, meaning those who engineered the coup, "upon the recommendation of not less than five Supreme Councilors."

This compact body of military officers was to exercise all legislative powers, including the authority to adopt the budget bill by a majority vote with a quorum of two-thirds of the councilors. Theoretically, therefore, seven military officers could adopt a budget bill [2] for the entire nation if the size of the Supreme Council was kept at twenty officers. For other legislative actions, the minimum number required was only six officers, since the Council could act by a majority vote, the simple majority of the councilors seated constituting the quorum.

The powers of the Council in regard to executive matters were equally sweeping. All the executive functions were to be performed by a cabinet under complete control of the Council. The Head of Cabinet, or the Prime Minister, was to be appointed by the Council, and he in turn would appoint cabinet members "with the approval of the Supreme Council." The cabinet had to assume collective responsibility to the Supreme Council, which could remove cabinet members *en bloc* by a two-thirds vote of the councilors seated. The Council could remove a cabinet member by a simple majority vote.

The judicial branch was placed under similar control by the Supreme Council. The Chief Justice and the justices of the Supreme Court were to be appointed by the President upon the recommendation of the Council. The assignment of other judges, including the chiefs of district courts, were to be made by the Chief Justice with the approval of the Supreme Council.

Other important matters that required decisions by the Supreme Council included proclamation and termination of martial law; appointment and removal of the chairman of the Joint Chiefs of Staff, and the Chief of Staff of each armed force; and approval of appointment of the prosecutor-general, the chairman of the Board of Audit, the chairman of the Inspection Commission, the presidents of National Universities, ambassadors and ministers, and managers of important government-operated enterprises. The appointments of provincial governors, the mayor of Seoul Special City, and the mayor of a city with a population of not less than 150,000, were to be made by the cabinet with the approval of the Supreme Council.

The crowning touch to the thorough concentration of power in a single and compact ruling body was added by the following provision in Article 11 of the Law Regarding Extraordinary Measures for National Reconstruction: "When the President (of the Republic) is in default or unable to perform his duties for any reason, his powers shall successively be exercised by the Chairman of the Supreme Council for National Reconstruction, the Vice-Chairman thereof and the Head of Cabinet." As early as June 6, 1961, therefore, President Yun was given public notice that he was dispensable. Yun, however, stayed on.

The Supreme Council for National Reconstruction comprised thirty members and two advisers, as of May 20, when the body acquired the new name. The military ranks of the members ranged from lieutenant colonels to lieutenant generals, nineteen out of the thirty being generals. Three supreme councilors were Marine Corps officers, one each from the Air Force and the Navy, and all the rest from the Army. The two advisers were retired military officers.[3]

That about a third of the supreme councilors were lieutenant colonels and colonels, mostly in their thirties, was a reflection of the substantial contribution made by these young officers to the cause of the military revolution. Their resolve, energy, and dedication had often been crucial elements in the successful execution of the revolution, and evidently they had earned their powerful positions in the "supreme governing organ" of the nation. Appointments to Council committees, the real power centers within the Council, revealed the relatively dominant position of the "Young Turks" in the "main force of the revolution." Supreme Council Order No. 4 made appointments to fourteen committees, nine of which were headed by lieutenant colonels and colonels [4]—most of them members of the "eighth graduating class" of the Korean Military Academy. The five-man special committee on personnel affairs, appointed on May 27, was headed by Major General Yi Chu-il, an influential leader in the Council, but three out of the five members were from the "eighth graduating class." Thus a majority vote in this important special committee, which would presumably play a decisive role in the exercise of the enormous appointive and removal powers of the Council, belonged to a colonel and two lieutenant colonels.

The youthful character of the ruling elite was certainly a significant development. The abundance of fresh blood and energy that now characterized the military regime was a far cry from the composition of the Rhee and Chang regimes, in which older men, often in their sixties, were very much in evidence. Suddenly, a new generation occupied positions of overwhelming power. This fact was at once a strength and a weakness for the military junta as a ruling body. If the freshness and rawness of the new elite promised a surge of vitality, it also meant lack of experience in politics and lack of sophistication in the intricate art of governing.

As the locus of the real power center gradually emerged, a flurry of activities began. Grim-faced military officers, often in their fatigues, scurried about, and army jeeps rushed to and fro in the crowded streets of the capital. A fourteen-man cabinet was appointed. All except one of them were active military officers, ranging in rank from colonel to lieutenant general—the exception being the foreign minister, a retired three-star general. Six of the fourteen were members of the Supreme Council. Of the provincial governors and mayors of principal cities appointed by Supreme Council Order No. 11, nine were brigadier generals and nine were colonels.[5] These appointments appeared to set a pattern of subsequent appointments by the military junta.

All public officials and employees of the government, of government-run enterprises, and of such organizations as banks were ordered by the junta to work seven days a week. Even faculty members of public universities and colleges and the teaching staff of other public school systems were ordered to work all days of the week, though there were to be no classes on Sundays. Supreme Council Order No. 5, addressed to all officers and men of the military, prohibited drinking of any alcoholic beverages during working hours and also prohibited their patronage of "restaurants, dance halls, billiard halls, and tea-houses." [6]

Supreme Council Decree No. 6, issued on May 22, stipulated that "all political parties and social organizations" must be disbanded by the following day. Other apolitical organizations, such as academic societies, religious organizations, and those engaged in social work, had to register by May 31. On the day that all political parties and social organizations were suddenly and completely decreed out of existence throughout South Korea, Supreme Council Decree No. 11 specified that publishing of newspapers be limited to those with complete printing facilities for the production of newspapers and that news services be limited to those with complete wire service facilities for transmission and reception. Strange as it might seem, this simple decree led to the cancellation by the Ministry of Public Information of the licenses of 834 newspapers, news services, and other periodicals. The remaining media of mass communication were placed under "self-censorship." [7] It should be pointed out that many of the banned papers and news services were financially dubious and had tended to support themselves through blackmail. In any case, South Korea suddenly became a hushed country.

At the same time, known "corrupt elements" in the government began to be cashiered, and an announcement reported that about 41,000 of the 240,989 civil servants would be dismissed. It was charged that many of them had secured their sinecures through nepotism, favoritism, or bribery during the Rhee and Chang periods.[8] "Gangsters and hoodlums" were arrested and were paraded about the streets of Seoul, many of them displaying signs—in the fashion of sandwichmen— which read: "I was a hoodlum." At the same time, arrests of "leftists" and of officers who did not support the coup, including General Yi Han-lim of the First Army, were carried out.

According to a publication by the Foreign Ministry under the military junta:

Assistance has been given to farmers: arrangements have been made for the repayment of usurious loans at reasonable interest rates over a period of time; vitally needed fertilizer has been distributed, at the established price, for the first time in the history of the Republic. The payment of the annual farm subsidies was announced on one day, and on the following day payments were made by county offices to farmers in full. (In the past, such payments were delayed for six or more months—and in the end the farmers were lucky if they received half of the amount, the rest having disappeared by what might be called a process of osmosis into the pockets of officials all down the line.)

Tax evaders have been located, and legal processes to enforce payment of delinquent and evaded taxes initiated. (One group of 15 businessmen alone has publicly admitted evading the *Hwan* equivalent of more than $33,449,924.00 in income taxes, and has voluntarily offered all restitution plus penalties.) Such evasions, of course, were possible only through massive bribery of public officials.

Law is being enforced. It is no longer possible to bribe police or prosecutors. Malefactors, rich or poor, receive the same treatment from the police and the courts.[9]

While the public was dazzled at these developments and claims, the Supreme Council for National Reconstruction Law, which also established the Central Intelligence Agency, was followed by the Central Intelligence Agency Law of June 10. Article 18 of the former law stipulated: "A Central Intelligence Agency shall be established under the Supreme Council for the purpose of countering indirect aggression of the Communist forces and to remove obstacles to the execution of the revolutionary tasks." The latter law specified that the Central Intelligence Agency was "to coordinate and supervise activities of government ministries, including armed forces, concerning information and investigation of matters at home and abroad related to the ensuring of national security and the investigation of criminal activities."[10] It was then headed by Colonel Kim Chong-p'il, a central figure among "the main force of the revolution" and a member of the class of 1949 of the Korean Military Academy.

These steps were followed by the Revolutionary Court and Prosecution Law. The cases that could be tried by the court established by this law included those relating to the disposition of illicit funds and punishment of election irregularities. The machinery for indicting and punishing those frowned on by the military regime was completed by a series of special laws, including the one legalizing the arrest of "anti-state criminals" without warrants, and the Anti-Communist Law, which was, according to W. D. Reeve, "so framed that anyone might be accused under it and providing for the reward of informers." [11] The junta now had the apparatus for policing and eliminating elements inimical to the military regime.

After providing itself with this official apparatus, the revolutionary leaders set about removing those within the military regime whose presence and support were no longer needed. The first major target of the purges was no other than General Chang To-yŏng—Chairman of the Supreme Council, Chief of Cabinet, Minister of Defense, and Army Chief of Staff. Seemingly, General Chang had occupied the most powerful position in the military junta, in the cabinet, and in the army. Because he was the Army Chief of Staff at the time of the coup, his acceptance—though extremely hesitant—of the chairmanship of the Military Revolutionary Committee and subsequently of the Supreme Council contributed greatly in creating the impression that the entire army was behind the coup. But Chang had wavered for almost a day following the coup before he threw his lot in with the revolutionaries, who neither respected nor trusted him.[12]

It was announced on June 6 that he had "released" the posts of Chief of Staff and Minister of Defense and on July 3 that he had "resigned" from the positions of Chairman of the Supreme Council and Chief of Cabinet. At the same time, three supreme councilors were also dropped from the junta. Thereafter there were persistent rumors of General Chang's arrest, which was officially announced on July 8, when it was stated that he and forty-five others had been captured on July 3 as they were engaged in an antirevolutionary "plot" to assassinate the "main force of the revolution." [13]

General Park, the real mastermind of the military revolution, who was content to remain as Vice-Chairman of the Supreme Council as long as such an arrangement was politic, assumed the chairmanship of the Council in name as well as in reality on July 3. At the same time General Song Yo-ch'an, who had returned from the United States and become Defense Minister, was appointed Chief of Cabinet.

General Song, or "Tiger Song," was hardly a member of "the main force of the revolution." He had been in Washington, D.C., on the day of the coup and had no direct liaison with those who led it. Even before he could ascertain the composition of the Military Revolutionary Committee, however, General Song issued a strongly worded statement from Washington supporting the coup.[14] It was probably a characteristic action of "Tiger Song." At a time when the relationship between the Military Revolutionary Committee and the United States government was a matter of grave concern, the timely and unreserved support voiced by General Song, known to a goodly number of Americans since the Korean War, was welcome news to revolutionary leaders in Seoul. And when they sought a suitable replacement for Lieutenant General Chang To-yŏng, retired Lieutenant General Song Yo-ch'an was available. As long as Premier and Defense Minister Song did not harbor political ambitions of his own, he could be useful to the revolutionary government. Furthermore, he was better known within Korea as well as abroad than most other members of the revolutionary nucleus.

By the end of the seventh week following the coup, the political and governmental structure had undergone fundamental upheavals. The democratic polity of the Second Republic—at least in terms of theory—was now completely discredited and discarded. The representative superstructure had been decreed out of existence, as were most freedoms. A highly centralized, tightly regimented, and almost omnipotent military regime emerged under the undisputed leadership of General Chung Hee Park. These seven weeks may be called the first phase of the consolidation of "the main force of the revolution."

General Park: The Man and His Ideas

With the purge of General Chang, the position of General Chung Hee Park as undisputed chieftain of the revolutionary government became glaringly evident. Even when General Park occupied the vice-chairmanship of the Supreme Council, observers had sensed that he was the central figure of the military junta. Now that the thin veil of diarchy had been discarded, attention had to be focused on the slim, taciturn, and unsmiling general, normally clad in fatigues. There was but limited value in a scrutiny of institutions that were undergoing such dizzying changes; an understanding of the chieftain and his ideas was to be far more valuable in comprehending the revolutionary movement and government.

It is immediately clear that General Park's background is strikingly different from that of President Rhee or Premier Chang. To be sure, Rhee and Chang were quite different in terms of personality, temperament, and approaches to, and exercise of, political power. There were, however, certain basic similarities between them. Both were Christians, though Rhee was a Methodist and Chang a Catholic. Both were born in the nineteenth century, though Rhee was much older than Chang. Both had at least intellectual commitment to the representative form of government. Both were urbane, civil, and cultured. Finally, both were Western-educated heirs to the aristocratic or landed class of traditional Korea.

Chung Hee Park was born into an extremely poor farming family in a tiny village of some ninety households. The boy born on September 30, 1917, was the youngest among five sons and two daughters of Pak (Park) Sŏng-bin, then fifty-four, and Paek Nam-i, then forty-four. As young Chung Hee grew, it soon became apparent that he was physically shorter and slighter than other children.[15] Like most other villagers of Sangmo-ri, in Kyŏngsang-pukdo, a southeastern province of Korea, the Park family eked out a scanty livelihood on the sterile, dry fields located at the foot of Mount Kŭmo.[16] Chung Hee's birthplace was a small, mud-walled, thatch-roofed house —where his oldest brother still lives.

Children of Sangmo-ri, which could hardly afford even a one-room school, had to attend a grammar school, or a "common school" as they were called, more than three miles away. All of them had to walk to school, often unprotected from the drenching rains or knee-deep snow. Most pupils walked together in a group, but not Chung Hee. Because he excelled in his work, he was recommended by the common school to enter a normal school in Taegu, the provincial capital. Normal schools then trained common-school teachers. They gave relatively inexpensive, terminal, vocational training to bright but poor students, most of whom were satisfied to build a career as common-school teachers. Chung Hee evidently received occasional financial assistance from his much older brothers and was graduated from the normal school in 1937.

Then followed two years of teaching at the primary school of Mungyŏng, a small town in Kyŏngsang-pukdo. He sent a part of his meager salary of 35 yen each month to his home in Sangmo-ri. After two years of teaching children in a sleepy provincial town, Teacher Park had had enough.

He entered the Military Academy of Manchukuo, the puppet state of militarist Japan, in 1940. Training at the Academy was a path for some ambitious young Koreans to become members of the officer corps of the imperial Japanese army. Upon graduation from the Military Academy in Tokyo in 1944, Park was assigned to the Japanese army in Manchuria (the Kwantung Army) as a second lieutenant, until the Japanese surrender only about a year after his commissioning. "Little is known about his life in this period," [17] because Park seldom talks about his activities in the imperial Japanese army.

When he was discharged from the defeated army, he quietly returned to his home village as a house guest of his older brothers. It was a year of depression and frustration. Park was jobless, virtually penniless, and had little to occupy himself with beyond indulging in heavy drinking at the expense of his accommodating friends.[18] After graduating from two military academies and after the experience as an officer in the "Imperial Army," he probably had little desire to return to a tame life of grammar-school teaching. Even if he desired it, Korean schools, which were then administered by highly nationalistic men, might not have welcomed a former Japanese army officer as a teacher. Yet he was not trained for any other vocation.

It was predictable that he would join the newly organized South Korean constabulary, as did many of his contemporaries with similar military backgrounds. His life as a melancholy loafer came to an end when he entered the Korean Military Academy in September, 1946. In view of his previous training, he was graduated in the same year with a rank of captain. Thus he resumed the military career that he had begun at about the age of twenty-three.

Until the *coup d'état,* his career was one of steady, if not spectacular, rises through the ranks of the rapidly expanding armed forces, except for one period when he was reportedly sentenced to death by a court martial after being accused of association with Communist insurrectionists of the Yŏsu-Sunchŏn rebellion of October, 1948.[19] The Rhee administration had launched a determined campaign of liquidation of

Communist elements within the South Korean military forces, and it is said that Park saved his life by cooperating with the government in the campaign. He was reinstated in the officer corps of the South Korean army at about the time of the outbreak of the Korean War.

Park remarried in December, 1950, only about half a year after the outbreak of the Korean War, at the age of thirty-three. His first marriage to a country girl had been an "arranged marriage" to satisfy the wishes of his aging mother. He had been only about seventeen years old at the time, still attending the Taegu Normal School. That marriage had broken up when he left Sangmo-ri to embark upon his military career.[20] By his second marriage, he has two daughters and a son.

By 1953, the last year of the Korean War, Park had advanced to the rank of brigadier general, at the age of thirty-six, a relatively young age even in the Korean Army, noted for the youth of its generals. As an artillerist, Brigadier General Park attended the advanced course of the U.S. Army Artillery School at Fort Sill, Oklahoma, returning to Korea for assignment as Commandant of the Artillery School of the Korean Army. From this post he was transferred to the Fifth Infantry Division as Commanding General, which post he held until 1957, when he attended the Command and General Staff College of the Korean Army. After tours as Deputy Commanding General of the Sixth Army Corps and Commanding General of the Seventh Infantry Division, he was promoted to the rank of Major General in 1958 and assigned to be Chief of Staff, First Army. Since 1959, he has filled the following assignments: Commanding General, Sixth Military District Command; Commanding General, Logistics Base Command; Commanding General, First Military District

Command; Deputy Chief of Staff for Operations, Korean Army Headquarters; and Deputy Commanding General, Second Army.

Throughout his military career, he had been known for almost total absence from the gay social functions attended by most high-ranking government and military officers, their American counterparts, and American military advisers. While many young, dashing Korean Army generals conspicuously enjoyed their newly won social positions since the Korean War, General Park was an exception. He was never a great mixer, social functions being too rich for his blood; and he did not particularly enjoy petty salon politics. He had never played a game of golf with American personnel in Korea.[21]

For various reasons, Major General Park was a little-known figure when he suddenly emerged as the mastermind of the military revolution. After becoming the powerful chairman of the Supreme Council for National Reconstruction, he was twice promoted in a matter of months: to the rank of lieutenant general in August, 1961, and to the rank of general in November of the same year.

Political ideas of Chung Hee Park can be gleaned from a few brief writings somewhat hastily published under his name after the coup. The three most important of these treatises are *Chidojado* (The Ways of a Leader), *Uri minjokŭi nagalkil* (The Path for Our Nation), and *Kukkawa hyŏngmyŏngkwa na* (The Country, the Revolution and I).[22]

It is noteworthy that the thirty-five-page *Chidojado*, the first treatise to bear Park's name and published in the year of the *coup d'état*, was a highly personal discourse on "the ways of a leader." This treatise, which might have discussed any number of other pressing problems, probably was a reflection of a preoccupation of the leader of the Supreme

Council for National Reconstruction—the establishment of an effective leadership. A leader "must be heroic," General Park asserts, particularly in a revolutionary era. He believes that the qualifications for such a leader should be a consciousness of comradeship, the ability to judge and solve problems, foresight, dedication to principles or conscientious character, decisiveness, belief in democracy, conviction in one's goals, sincerity and passion, and trustworthiness.[23] These qualifications, with the exception of the "belief in democracy," are quite general attributes of any leader, or a heroic leader. For the purpose of *Chidojado*, his inclusion of "belief in democracy" was notable.

His discussion of the "belief in democracy" is brief, about seventeen lines in the Korean text.[24] He claims that the 1961 *coup d'état* was to "overthrow the anti-democratic system" of the Second Republic and to lay down the foundation for a "true, free democracy" in Korea. He declares that the coup was "certainly not for the establishment of a new dictatorship and totalitarianism." The leader

must be brave in combating dictatorship, including the communist dictatorship. Leaders must always breathe together with the people of the nation and must exert the maximum effort to infuse the people with the spirit of true freedom and democracy.[25]

The pamphlet projects an image of a heroic leader, divining the soul of the nation, inspiring them and resolutely guiding them toward the exalted goals of "true freedom and democracy." These terms—"true freedom and democracy"—are used frequently, but since they are not defined in the pamphlet, the meanings attached to them by General Park have to be gleaned from his other treatises.

The leader of the military *coup d'état* raises a question in *The Ways of a Leader:* Was the military revolution inimical

to principles of "free democracy"? General Park asserts meta-
phorically that the military revolution was "a sort of a surgical operation" to save the nation. When a person or a nation
becomes ill, a doctor may restrict and regulate the activities of
the patient, may order his hospitalization, and may even force
an operation. "A surgical operation is not a merry amusement
but a sacrifice of a part in order to save the whole. It is, therefore, accepted as a necessary evil." [26] General Park evidently
posited himself as the doctor who made the diagnosis and
performed the operation.

As an exposition of General Park's political philosophy,
the second treatise, *The Path for Our Nation*, appears to be
important. Since a translated summary of the work, bearing
the general's name, was published in English under the title
"Korean Political Philosophy: Administrative Democracy," [27]
the English version will be briefly examined here.

Typically, the general points his fingers at the outset at
"the enemy within and without"—the Communists and the
internal, inherent weaknesses of the Korean people. In order
to overcome the enemy, declares the general, a "national
awakening" must lead to the cleansing of "all negative national characters." According to the translated summary:

Loyalty to the leaders, superior egotism and an extremely realistic
way of thinking were all negative national character. How can
one expect the growth of positive national character amongst
such a lack of patriotism and negative attitude which have been
implanted in us for so long. Patriotism and national consciousness
revived and national and people's revolution is just beginning.
One can cite "privilege" consciousness as the most important
element in preventing our common interests, prosperity and integrity. Clanism, factionalism and consciousness of family background can be said to have captured our thinking. One can justify
this if such opposition conflicts originated from a difference in

ideals, yet when we closely examine the origins, these are all the direct result of trying to get hegemony and wealth. When we are aware that we are one people there can be no "privilege" consciousness.[28]

Because of the inherent, historical weakness of the Korean people, General Park proclaims, the nation must aim at nothing less than "the reformation of man." The military coup was to be the beginning of a military revolution that must lead to a national and social revolution that cannot be completed short of "the reformation of man." It was to be a gigantic task.

In his conception of democracy, General Park shows strong evidences of preoccupation with economic equality. He emphasizes that without economic equality democracy is no more than an "abstract, useless concept." Park proclaims that unless economic equality is guaranteed "by establishing a welfare state" in Korea, the Koreans "will have to face another crisis" [29]—possibly meaning another military revolution. (Exactly the same declaration is repeated in his third treatise: "We can only march ahead with a single-hearted determination to establish a welfare state in the Orient.") [30]

Park then observes that most countries in Asia "have to resort to undemocratic and extraordinary measures" in order to improve the living conditions of the masses. One cannot deny, according to Park, that the people "are more frightened of poverty and hunger than totalitarianism." [31] He observes that the social inheritance of most Asian countries favors "oligarchy" and that "roots of democracy" cannot be imported even if "forms of it" might be copied.

Having said all this, General Park still proclaims that the ultimate aim of the revolution is the establishment of genuine democracy. To make the attainment of the ultimate aim possible, "the road to follow during the revolutionary period and its nature must be democratic because there can be no future without the present. . . . Thus, I feel the democracy we have to practice during this revolutionary period is not that of the West but that which is suited to our society and political conditions. This I call administrative democracy." [32]

Since little popular foundation of democracy exists in Korea, the revolutionary regime must uphold democratic principles at least at the administrative level. Administrative democracy practiced during the revolutionary or transitional period must allow and welcome criticisms and recommendations by the people. All the achievements and failures of the administration should be judged by the public. The general also proclaims that the revolutionary forces must democratize the administrative structure in the direction of decentralization to encourage individual initiative and administrative efficiency. "The administrative revolution, the democratization of administration, must be achieved by rational management as well as effective democratic control." But he does not explain here how "effective democratic control" is to be achieved. Nor does he elaborate here how the military revolutionaries, who have known little but regimentation, discipline, and unquestioned chains of command, propose to democratize the civilian administration. Once the administration is democratized, is it then expected to democratize the nation? Obviously, the answer is affirmative: "This revolutionary period can be said to be an educational period to create a national spirit conducive to the enjoyment of democracy, an enlightening period to raise and develop independent abilities of the people." [33] These ideas are akin to the familiar notions of the tutelage period and of guided democracy.

The Country, the Revolution and I was published over two years after the coup in the name of General Park, still the chairman of the junta. The revolutionary soldier again justifies the military takeover and extols the accomplishments of the military regime, explaining away the failure of the military to restore the government to civilians as had been proclaimed to the world in the "revolutionary pledges."

Over two years after the coup, the general is again declaring that "the revolution must be accomplished." He is still expounding on the essence of the revolution and attacking the "reactionary elements": "The purpose of this revolution was to reconstruct the nation and establish a self-sustaining economy, but its essential purpose was to restore to all the people the political and economic systems which had become the possession of a few privileged classes," [34] or the reactionary elements.

The revolution, according to the general, was to form "a new force for the age." The new force was to become "a new face to farmers, fishermen, laborers and small citizens, intent on establishing a common people's government, common people's economy and common people's culture." [35] The revolution was to enable "a new elite" to take over the nation, and the revolution had to mean "a turnover of generation."

Park showed his utmost contempt and abhorrence of the politicians in the Rhee and Chang periods by calling them the "trash—the old politicians." [36] By the military revolution,

their bastion was being breached and their very lives were threatened. It was natural that they should be desperate. Like a household heirloom, they brandished ostensible democracy. This was their tactic-only, a smoke-screen. But such a "world of night" is over. It is bound to be over. . . .

The revolutionary government will not make freedom the monopoly of certain classes only, as these others were wont to do when they took over power. Democracy is not their exclusive monopoly or patent right. They were profiteers, stole and sold freedom, wholesale and retail! . . .

The misfortune of rule by special classes should not be repeated again in our society.

We can only march ahead with a single-hearted determination to establish a welfare state in the Orient, in which justice has its way, in which truth breathes, in which activity and newness are rewarded and in which hope and ideals abound.[37]

The most prominent and recurrent theme in his political theories appears to be his detestation of the privileged class, the reactionary elements, the "trash." The revolution must produce a turnover of generation, or a new ruling elite, headed by a heroic leader who will resolutely guide the masses to the promised land of democracy. Given the fact that the revolution was executed by the military, with its normal attributes, the nature and composition of the new elite could be inferred without much difficulty. To what extent the general's repeated reference to genuine democracy was meaningful had to await the actual behavior of the military government under the undisputed control of General Park.

The Purges and Their Aftermath

After consolidating the military junta by expelling unreliable elements in military uniform from their positions of power, the junta turned its attention to the purge of the "remnants of the old order," or what General Park called the "trash." The military rulers proclaimed that they had to clean up the "political and social evils of the past" in order to lay the foundation for "national renaissance and reconstruction." The period of the "purification" and consolidation of the military government began in August, 1961, about a month after Park became the Chairman of the Supreme Council, and lasted for about a year.

The military government initiated the purification operation by confiscating over 5,752,000,000 *won* from fifty-nine "illicit fortune makers" [38] who allegedly had amassed their fortunes through illegal means under the Chang and Rhee regimes. Having boosted the prestige of General Park through his visit to the United States and Japan in November, 1961, the military government then promulgated, on March 16, 1962, the sweeping Political Activities Purification Law,[39] banning political activities by "old politicians" of all conceivable types—including the Liberals, Democrats, New Democrats, and leaders of progressive organizations—for six years, until August 15, 1968.

The twelve-article law defined political activities as follows: becoming a candidate in a public election; delivering campaign speeches for or against candidates; promoting or preparing for formation of political or social organizations; becoming a member of political or social organizations; becoming a sponsor or speaker for a political assembly; and promoting or obstructing political activities by politicians, political parties, and social organizations.

The law provided for the establishment of a seven-man Political Purification Committee to be appointed by the Supreme Council Chairman from among the supreme councilors. The committee was to screen those subject to the ban, which also affected numerous high government officials at the central and provincial levels, heads and staff of state-run enterprises under the Chang government, in addition to "notorious Liberals." Lieutenant General Yi Chu-il, Vice-Chairman of the Supreme Council, headed the committee.[40] Those who were declared to be subject to the ban could petition the Political Purification Committee for screening within fifteen days after public notice of their names was given to demonstrate their innocence. Otherwise, they were to be subject to the restriction of the law automatically.

About two weeks after the promulgation of the purification law, the Supreme Council made a series of dramatic announcements listing 4,369 persons as political figures who would be automatically barred from political activities unless they appealed for screening and were cleared by the Purification Committee. The staggering list, topped by Syngman Rhee and Chang Myŏn, included practically every single notable of the Second Republic and numerous Liberals of the First Republic. A conspicuous exception was President Yun Po-sŏn.

The 102-page roster issued by the Supreme Council attempted to blacklist a whole generation of "old politicians," at a time when thoughts of elections as a means of transferring the government to civilians were recurring in many minds. It had been already announced by General Park himself at a news conference on August 2, 1961, that "the turnover of the government to civilian control is planned to be in the summer of 1963." All political and social organizations had been liquidated immediately after the coup; now a generation of individual politicians was to be barred from political activity.

Of the 2,958 who petitioned the Purification Committee for screening, 1,336 were cleared. The clearance of applicants was based on many factors, including meritorious service in the cause of the military revolution, evidence that past misdeeds were performed under duress, evidence of repentance—as judged by seven soldiers of the Purification Committee. Political activities by over three thousand better-known figures were still banned when the Purification Committee completed the screening on May 30, 1962.

The bitter criticism of the purification measures and of the self-righteousness of the military rulers became uproarious even under stern revolutionary government. Former Premier Chang, for instance, was quoted as having said that the purification law "would do the basic principles of democracy great harm, because it is very likely to make the forthcoming general election a one-sided affair." [41] Even President Yun, who was exempt from the provisions of the law, resigned in protest on March 22, 1962. Pressures mounted on one man, General Park, who could, according to Article 9 of the law, pardon politicians regardless of whether applications for screening were made to the Purification Committee.

Accusations of the military rulers became increasingly vociferous as it became apparent that the military regime was failing to produce any economic miracles. Chairman Park gradually exercised his prerogative under Article 9, and when the ban on political activity was finally lifted on January 1, 1963, all but seventy-four political figures, including Syngman Rhee and Chang Myŏn, were pardoned and were able to resume political activities. Though the "purification measures" succeeded in humiliating, demoralizing, and further dividing "old politicians," as brooms in the hands of the soldiers, they failed to clean up the "trash."

General Park wrote in July, 1963: "The revolutionary government, having purified the political world as the primary step, concentrated its energy on economic improvement as the second step." [42] The junta had declared in its revolutionary pledges that: "We shall provide relief for poverty-stricken and hungry people, and devote our entire energies toward the development of a self-sustaining economy." The Five-Year Economic Development Plan of 1962–1966 was launched with fanfare shortly after the 1961 coup with the ambitious goal of increasing the gross national product by 40.7 per cent, an average annual increase of 7.1 per cent. In view of the fact that the gross national product had increased only 5.2 per cent in 1959 and 2.1 per cent in 1960, the plan seemed to have more "the nature of an aspiration than a precise economic document." [43] Many observers agreed that the five-year plan was an outgrowth of a blueprint—with politically inspired figures—drawn up by the Chang regime.

To finance the enormous investment required for the plan, the regime relied on United States aid and private donations for 42 per cent of the total, on governmental and private borrowing from abroad for 16 per cent.[44] More than one half of the required investment, therefore, depended on sources over which the Korean government had little control. And just when foreign—particularly American—resources became so important, the United States, increasingly concerned with dollar drains, cut back its economic aid (see Table 3).

Table 3. American economic assistance to Korea

Year	Millions of dollars
1961	244.0
1962	170.5
1963	194.7
1964	154.4

Source: *Haptong nyŏngam* (Haptong Annual), 1965.

In an attempt to mobilize domestic capital for the five-year plan, the junta hastily enacted a currency reform on June 9, 1962. A freeze on bank deposits brought many medium and small businesses to a halt, and the junta had to relax its freeze eleven days later to get the economy moving again. Early in July the junta abandoned the freeze entirely. Meanwhile, the losses resulting from economic stagnation and impairment of confidence in the banks was said to have been far greater than the total frozen deposits obtained.[45]

Because the military government was still committed to the five-year plan under these circumstances, the regime decided to print more money. From 1961 to 1963, the currency in circulation in South Korea increased by 70.2 per cent, and this situation inevitably created an inflationary spiral, finally forcing the regime to modify the plan to place emphasis on stabilization instead of growth. These developments adversely affected the livelihood of the great majority of the people (see Table 4).

Table 4. Average annual wholesale indexes in Seoul

Year	Index (1960 = 100)
1961	113.2
1962	123.8
1963	149.3
1964	164.7

Source: *Haptong nyŏngam* (Haptong Annual), 1965.

Though the regime promised a "miracle on the Han River" in the fashion of the "miracle on the Rhine" [46]—spectacular economic growth similar to that of war-devastated West Germany—an economic miracle could not be decreed by a military junta. Partly thanks to the annual increase rate of 2.9 per cent in population, the per capita annual income of an average Korean actually dropped from $87.71 to $85.25 during the year following the coup.[47]

Worse still, large-scale scandals—the so-called "Saenara Datsun automobile cases" and the "stock market manipulations"—involving leading members of the junta were uncovered. It was reported that vast sums of money had been swindled in the course of importing "Saenara automobiles," in fact the Japanese Datsuns, and suspicions were openly expressed that the windfall created by the stock market manipulations by leading figures of the junta was being used for the clandestine organization of the nucleus of a political party, which would become a vehicle for the military in seeking domination of the promised civilian government.[48]

The military had declared in the revolutionary pledges: "We shall eliminate corruption, and eradicate other social evils which had become prevalent in our country." They had harped loudly on the corruption and evils from previous governments that they were going to eradicate, and had been boastful of their discipline and honesty. The revelation of their own corruption and manipulations at the expense of the people dealt a blow to the prestige and reputation of the military regime. With the realization that the government was not practicing what it preached so self-righteously, the people became disillusioned and remarked aloud that the "new evils" were more brazen than the "old evils." The military rulers now earnestly searched their souls, groping for the best posture for facing the future.

Chapter 7

The Politics of Restoration

The sixth revolutionary pledge promised that the military rulers would restore the government to "honest and conscientious civilians" and would return to their "proper military duties." While announcing on August 2, 1961, that the turnover of the government to "civilian control" was planned for the summer of 1963, General Park also declared that a "new constitution" would be promulgated by March, 1963, and that a general election would be held the following May, so that the government would be "completely turned over to civilian control" in accordance with the provisions of the Constitution. Chairman Park added that political activities, presumably by civilians, would be "tolerated in early 1963" just before the general election.[1]

Thus questions of when and how the restoration of civilian government would occur were answered by General Park himself in his carefully prepared statement read at one of his rare news conferences. The text of the brief statement, which was reproduced as a United Nations document and in *American Foreign Policy: Current Documents*,[2] also contained three ringing phrases, asserting that the revolutionary government was endeavoring to establish "the foundation for new democratic institutions," to create "a true democratic political or-

der," and to establish "a firm foundation for democratic prosperity of the nation."

Despite the answers given in the general's statement, numerous questions remained. Who would be regarded as honest and conscientious civilians by the military rulers who evidently considered a whole generation of politicians as corrupt
and inefficient? How could civilian politicians who had been
disorganized, blackballed, humiliated, and straitjacketed by
political purification measures organize themselves again in
"early 1963" to face a general election in May? What were
the real intentions of "the main forces of the revolution"
around General Park? What were the soldiers who had
planned and executed the *coup d'état,* and now ran the country, doing to ensure their future after the termination of the
military rule?

The Zigzag to Restoration

While civilian politicians were stunned and paralyzed by
the promulgation of the Political Activities Purification Law
in March, 1962, a well-cloaked embryo of a political party
was already being formed. The clandestine but well-financed
organization once displayed a signboard of the Oriental Chem-
ical Company, Ltd., in a back alley of Seoul.[3] By the end of
March, 1963, the organization had already acquired a solid
nucleus. Members of the nucleus, including young professors,
writers, and some government officials, then received special
instructions on organizational techniques and methods of in-
doctrination at a training center.[4] The Center secretly trained
organizers for the capital area in April and May and those
for various provincial and local levels in June and July. By
October, 1962, the "underground organization" was already
prepared to recruit members on a large scale through methodi-

cal screening by the central secretariat in Seoul and numerous provincial and local secretariats. Recruitment of known political figures was handled by Kim Chong-p'il himself.[5] While "old politicians" were immobilized by the "political activities purification" measures, a tightly organized political party was being readied for unveiling in "early 1963."

Meanwhile, on July 11, 1962, the Supreme Council formed a constitutional deliberation committee comprising nine supreme councilors and twenty-one civilian advisers and experts. The committee quickly decided to amend the old constitution instead of drafting a "new constitution," as General Park had announced on August 2, 1961. A complete revocation of the old constitution would have raised a serious legal problem, the committee reasoned. The old constitution had been enacted by the First National Assembly, a body duly constituted through a U.N.-sponsored general election, and was the basis on which rested the recognition accorded the government of the Republic of Korea.[6] As had been the case with the presidency of the Second Republic, the revolutionary government indicated a peculiar sensitivity to a legal point.

Accordingly, the Supreme Council simply revised Article 9 of the Law Concerning the Extraordinary Measures for National Reconstruction to stipulate that constitutional amendments adopted by the Supreme Council would be considered valid if a majority of the vote was registered in favor of such amendments on a referendum participated in by at least a majority of voters. While maintaining a façade of legality and continuity, the junta proceeded to draft an essentially new constitution,[7] the main features of which will be discussed briefly in the subsequent section of this chapter because they provide the institutional basis for the present Third Republic.

In about three and a half months after the organization of the committee, it had completed drafting a series of far-reaching amendments to the constitution. In August the committee held a public hearing for a week on the proposed constitutional amendments, "to mirror public opinion on the basic law." By the end of October the committee had finished its work, and on November 3 the Supreme Council unanimously approved the draft and formally proposed the amendments. Two days later Chairman Park placed them on a thirty-day public notice.

During the period of public notice, no less than thirteen supreme councilors undertook lecture tours to various parts of the country to focus attention on the proposed December 17 referendum, the first in the Korean history. Martial law, under which the Korean people had lived ever since May, 1961, was lifted on December 5, 1962, less than two weeks before the proposed referendum, "to relax the political atmosphere." Out of the total of 12,412,798 registered voters, 10,585,998, or 85.28 per cent, participated in the referendum. Of these participants, 8,339,333, or 78.78 per cent of the participants, voted in favor of the constitutional amendments, while 2,008,801 cast negative votes and 237,864 were listed as invalid.

Chairman Park, in his capacity as Acting President, formally promulgated the new, or amended, constitution on December 26. He declared that his nineteen-month-old government was "now even more encouraged and determined to carry out the revolutionary tasks and rebuild democracy" in Korea. He also said that "a new and shining tradition has been established." [8] Thus the Korean constitution, which had been revised twice during each of the two preceding regimes, had been rewritten extensively for the fifth time in the fourteen years of its existence.

On the day after the promulgation of the Constitution, General Park made an important public announcement: "Considering the political situation, we [supreme councilors] resolved that it is fit for us to retire from active (military) duty, and play an active role in the future civilian government." [9] The general, in a smartly tailored military uniform with four stars on each shoulder, told the press conference that views had been expressed favoring political participation by supreme councilors in the future government without taking off their uniforms. "Though this is possible, we decided to retire from active [military] duty so as to avoid setting an unsavory precedent in a free democracy."

General Park asserted that this decision was not a violation of the revolutionary pledges, "since we are not to automatically join the civilian government in military uniform." The Chairman of the Supreme Council also stated that the revolutionary government would revise the Law Concerning Extraordinary Measures "to enable [Supreme] Councilors to remain at their present posts after becoming civilians" [10] by the end of February, 1963. The sixth of the revolutionary pledges had read: "As soldiers, after we have completed our mission, we shall restore the government to honest and conscientious civilians, and return to our proper military duties." Evidently, the revolutionary soldiers themselves were to become honest and conscientious civilians by discarding their uniforms.

Though the position of General Park regarding the restoration of the civilian government zigzagged a number of times in the subsequent months, depending on whether the "hard line faction" or the "moderate faction" among the revolutionaries had the upper hand in the power alignment in and around the junta, his decision of December 27, 1962, and the reasoning behind it were to remain significant. The factional struggle between the hard-line group, which insisted on "participating in the civil rule," and the moderate group, which held that revolutionary soldiers had to be faithful to their own pledges, continued for some months. In fact, during periods of heated controversies within the military groups, there were indications that feuding factions in the ruling groups were preparing to mobilize armed units for a possible showdown.[11] In the end, however, the hard-line faction, or the "Kim-Hong-Kil line"—advocated by Kim Chong-p'il, Hong Chong-ch'ŏl, and Kil Chae-ho, all 1949 graduates of the Military Academy—won out, and it meant a return to Chairman Park's position of December 27.

The government also promulgated the Political Party Law,[12] the first of the kind in Korea, on December 31, 1962, to become effective on the following day. A political party could be launched, according to the law, only when a central chapter in the capital city and local chapters in more than one-third of election districts of the country had been formed. Since each chapter had to have more than fifty members, and since the election districts were to number about 120, the law made it mandatory for a political party to have over 2,000 registered members to engage in political activities when the ban against them was lifted just before the proposed 1963 elections. It was stated that this provision aimed at preventing emergence of splinter and progressive or leftist parties.

The law contained an unprecedented provision that the head of the political party claiming the largest number of opposition members in the National Assembly would be paid by the government the same allowance as that annually received by the House Speaker. The law prohibited financial contributions to political parties by foreigners and by several categories of organizations including state-run enterprises, banks and other financial organizations, labor unions, school foundations, and religious organizations.

The law also provided that a political party was subject to

dissolution by a Supreme Court decision. Once dissolved, former members of the body could not reorganize themselves into another political party under a party constitution similar to that of the defunct body. The law declared that parties were to enjoy freedom of activities within the scope of the Constitution and laws.

As "the year of the restoration of civil rule" dawned on the frigid Korean peninsula, the military government announced that the ban on political activities was lifted as of New Year's Day, 1963. The government at the same time released 171 former politicians from the restrictions of the political purification measures. This additional clearance of blacklisted politicians, however, left over 2,800 ex-politicians still banned from participating in political activities until August, 1968.

The first open meeting of sponsors for a pro-military political party, which had been clandestinely but methodically nurtured for a year under the direction of Kim Chong-p'il, was held on January 5, 1963. The new party, the Democratic Republican Party, officially came into being on January 18 and nominated Kim Chong-p'il as chairman of its preparatory committee. With the inauguration of the Democratic Republican Party, however, the factional strife within the military revolutionary groups, hitherto largely unknown to the public, became visible and ferocious.

Song Yo-ch'an, who had served in the military government as the Defense Minister, and subsequently Foreign Minister, and as Prime Minister, openly criticized General Park's intention to run in the forthcoming presidential elections. Marine General Kim Tong-ha, chairman of the Standing Committee of the Economic and Financial Committee of the Supreme Council, resigned on January 21 from his councilorship and membership in the preparatory committee of the

Democratic Republican Party. These dissensions marked the beginning of open clashes among the military rulers. Supreme Councilor Kim Chae-ch'un led the "moderates" in the Council who believed that the revolutionary soldiers should not participate in civil government. Defense Minister Pak Pyŏng-kwŏn was in agreement with the moderates.[13]

Meanwhile, those civilian politicians who had just been freed from the bondage of the Political Activities Purification Law scurried about to form their political parties. But instead of uniting themselves in a single opposition party against the Democratic Republican Party, which had already made decisive headway in the race, civilian politicians began to align themselves under two different political parties. The military government freed 273 influential ex-politicians from the blacklist on February 1. Hŏ Chŏng, one of those freed, promptly set about organizing still another opposition party.

The opposition groups directed their attacks against the military government. They protested loudly that the Democratic Republican Party was an illegal organization, having been formed while all civilian politicians were bound by the political purification measures. The opposition groups demanded the postponement of elections on the ground that they needed more time for preparation for the contest. Claiming that Chairman Park's candidacy for the presidency was a betrayal of the revolutionary pledges, they threatened to boycott the elections. They also demanded clear-cut criteria for the freeing of blacklisted civilian politicians. They charged that the military government was using the purification law to divide those opposition groups struggling to reorganize. Tensions mounted, threatening to explode.

The fiery and potentially dangerous antagonism between the hard-line faction and the moderate faction of the soldiers also generated white heat. Park then made a dramatic proposal on February 18 that he would stay out of the civil government to be established, postpone the elections scheduled for the spring, and completely lift the ban on all politicians—if all political parties would accept his conditions for these actions. The conditions included preventing reprisals against revolutionary soldiers after the establishment of a civil government; letting military officers run for public office or return to their military duties, according to individual choice; guaranteeing the status of those employed by the revolutionary government since the coup; the preservation of the new constitution; and cooperation in the Korean-Japanese negotiations on a suprapartisan basis.

These conditions were promptly accepted by civilian politicians, and a strangely solemn and emotion-charged ceremony was held in Citizens' Hall in Seoul on February 27 with Chairman Park, the Defense Minister, chiefs of staff of the armed services, and scores of leading civilian politicians attending. With their right hands raised, the former politicians swore to honor the military ruler's terms, and General Park, who appeared to be tearful at times, reaffirmed his promise not to take part in the civilian government and to release almost all politicians from political restriction. On the same day, 2,322 were stricken from the blacklist, leaving 269 on the list.

The United States government immediately and publicly welcomed General Park's decision to step out of the presidential elections. Official State Department spokesman Lincoln White said on the day after Park's announcement that it provided a basis for a "smooth transition to civilian government through the democratic processes in an atmosphere of national unity and stability." [14] The American Embassy in Seoul echoed White's statement. The United States, which had pressed the military rulers to return Korea to a civilian government, was evidently pleased with Park's announcement.

With Park's candidacy ruled out, civilian political parties began to grapple among themselves for dominance. Their internecine struggles again took on the appearance of an ugly, endless dogfight, reminiscent of the days preceding the coup. Then, on March 11, General Kim Chae-ch'un, who had replaced Kim Chong-p'il as director of the Central Intelligence Agency, announced that twenty anti-revolutionaries had been arrested for their plot to overthrow the military government. A few days after the announcement, on March 15, forty-five army officers and thirty-eight enlisted men staged a noisy demonstration in front of the Supreme Council building, General Park's headquarters.

The demonstrators in military uniform chanted their demand that General Park extend the military rule or take part in the presidential elections. Their obviously prepared slogans also demanded the dismissal of the Defense Minister, who had opposed Park's participation in the elections, execution of those arrested by the military government on charges of plotting a coup against the Park regime, immediate prohibition of political activities by "unconscientious" former politicians, and immediate proclamation of martial law. It was the first demonstration staged by military officers and men in uniform in the history of the Korean Army. Their chanting, immediately in front of the Supreme Council building, lasted for two hours before the demonstrators were "arrested."

The unprecedented soldiers' demonstration "created a crisis" that led to a series of "important conferences" and a "serious review of the situation." On the day following the demonstration, General Park made a startling announcement that the military junta had decided to extend military rule for four years. He then proposed a plebiscite in which the people would be given a chance to vote either "yes" or "no." At the same time, the military government banned once again all political activities and clamped censorship on the press under a law concerning "Temporary Measures Aimed at Settlement of Critical Situations." Former President Yun Po-sŏn bitterly stated that the general's new position "buried from this moment the democracy which had just begun budding." [15] Opposition political parties that were struggling to get on their feet were abruptly forced to cease their activities. The nation was rocked into panic.

It was soon reported that General Park had sent a letter to President Kennedy explaining his proposal for the four-year extension of military rule. After an ominous silence of several days, official State Department spokesman Lincoln White stated on March 25:

We believe that prolongation of military rule (in Korea) could constitute a threat to stable and effective government, and we understand that this whole matter is being reconsidered by the Korean government. . . . We hope that the junta and the major political groups in Korea can work out together a procedure for transmission to civilian government that will be acceptable to the nation as a whole.[16]

White added that he was certain that President Kennedy was aware of the U.S. policy behind the State Department's statement. Washington observers noted that the United States had once again stated its fundamental policy toward Korea clearly and firmly. They learned at the same time that the United States had flatly turned down the junta's request for an additional 25 million dollars in economic aid, "to underscore its determination to bring constitutional government in Korea." They emphasized that the White statement was made at that time to "correct any misapprehensions that the United States was in favor of continued rule by strong-man Gen. Chung

Hee Park and his military junta." [17] The U.S. Embassy immediately echoed the Washington statement, and American Ambassador Samuel D. Berger delivered on April 2 a reply from President Kennedy to General Park's letter.

General Park began to back down on April 8, when he declared that political activities were again permitted and the restrictions applied to the press lifted. On July 27, Park once again pledged that the transfer of government to civilians would be made within the year. These announcements marked the resumption of flurries of activity among all politicos, military and civilian, young and old.

The Civil Rule Party, which had emerged as a major rallying point for a large number of conservative ex-politicians, nominated former President Yun Po-sŏn as its presidential candidate. Yun, in accepting the nomination, was confident he could win because, he claimed, the people had been thoroughly alienated from the military government. The Party of the People, which was opposed to the military but failed to merge with the Civil Rule Party to form a united opposition against the military, nominated Hŏ Chŏng as its standard bearer. The Justice of the People Party, which had refused from the beginning to merge with the Party of the People, nominated Pyŏn Yŏng-t'e.

General Park resigned from active military service on August 30 and on the same day joined the Democratic Republican Party. On the very next day, he accepted the presidential nomination by the party that had been carefully prepared for the move under the direction of Kim Chong-p'il. The presidential elections were to be held on October 15, just a month and a half after General Park himself became an "honest and conscientious" civilian.

The arena of the presidential race was further crowded by the candidacy of retired General Song Yo-ch'an, by this time an archenemy of Park. The Free Democratic Party nominated Song shortly after he had been thrown into prison, largely for his severe and open criticism of Park. Other presidential candidates included Chang Yi-sŏk of the Newly Emerging Party, a completely new face in the nation's political scene, and O Chae-yŏng of the Autumn Wind Society, who had been a member of the National Assembly under the Liberal regime. When the registration period for candidates ended on September 15, only a month before the voting, seven candidates were running; one representing the military junta and its supporters, and the rest representing the divided opposition. The nation held its breath and wondered which one of them would give substance to the political system that was to emerge under the amended or the new constitution.

The Constitutional Framework

A discussion of the Constitution and the legal-institutional aspects of the government may not be the most fruitful way of understanding the political dynamics of an emergent nation or of gauging the degree of democratic development. It is true, however, that the oft-amended Constitution provides the basic structural framework for the government of the Third Republic. The Constitution also professes to reflect the basic principles on which the republic was to be founded.

Despite the sweeping series of amendments, the Constitution has retained in its first article ringing proclamations that "the Republic of Korea shall be a democratic republic" and that "the sovereignty of the Republic of Korea shall reside in the people and all state authority shall emanate from the people." It is further declared that "all public officials shall be servants of the entire people and shall be responsible to the people." [18]

Foremost among the main features of the new constitution is the restoration of a presidential system, somewhat similar to the one originally adopted by the Constitution of 1948. In fact, the position of the President became far stronger under the new constitution than under the First Republic. Under the new system the State Affairs Council (cabinet) has been downgraded to a consultative body that may "deliberate on important policies" (Article 83), whereas under the former system the State Affairs Council could "decide important state policy" (Article 68) at least in theory. This change reflects a revulsion felt by most Koreans against the cabinet system of the Second Republic, in which a weak executive was overridden by a strong legislature.

The President now appoints the Prime Minister without the National Assembly's concurrence. Members of the State Affairs Council are similarly appointed by the President upon the proposal of the Prime Minister, who may also recommend their removal to the President. The President may remove ministers as well as the Prime Minister, largely at his discretion. The National Assembly, also, may "advise" the President as to the removal of the Prime Minister or any member of the State Affairs Council, and here one may see a faint parallel to a legislature's nonconfidence vote against the cabinet. It might appear that the new constitution accommodates certain features of the cabinet system intended to counterbalance excessive authority that might devolve upon the President. Although the President is required to act on the National Assembly's recommendation for removal, he may refuse it, giving his "special reasons." Even this parallelism, therefore, does not last long.[19]

Because the President holds practically unlimited power to dismiss the Prime Minister and members of the State Affairs Council, the right of the Prime Minister and of the members of the State Affairs Council to countersign state documents or to participate in policy deliberations is utterly ineffective in curbing presidential powers. Furthermore, no vice-presidency is established under the new constitution. It provides a presidential system pure and simple. In the event that the President becomes incapacitated, a general election is to be held to choose his successor (Article 64). When the remaining tenure is less than two years, however, or less than one half of the four-year presidential term, the National Assembly elects the successor.

The second outstanding feature of the new constitution is the provision for a unicameral legislature. The constitutional amendment of 1952 called for a bicameral legislature, although it was only in 1960 that an upper house actually came into being. The military leaders were committed to promptness of governmental action and they naturally opted for a one-house legislature, "to represent the single will of the people." [20] To forestall the possibility of the National Assembly's causing continued harassment to the administration by staying in "permanent" session, Article 43 limits the period of a regular session and an extraordinary session to 120 days and 30 days respectively.

The executive branch is to formulate the budget for each fiscal year and submit it to the National Assembly, which has to decide on the budget within thirty days before the beginning of the fiscal year. If the budget is not adopted within that period, the executive may, within the limit of revenue and in conformity with the budget for the previous fiscal year, disburse the following expenditures until the adoption of the budget by the National Assembly: (1) the emolument of public officials and basic expenditures for the conduct of administration, (2) maintenance cost for agencies and institutions established by the Constitution or law and the obligatory expenditures provided by law, and (3) expenditures for continuous projects already provided in the budget (Article 50). Thus legislative control over the national budget is feeble indeed.

Bills may be introduced by the members of the National Assembly or by the executive branch. Furthermore, the Prime Minister, cabinet members, and other "representatives of the executive may attend meetings of the National Assembly or its committees to report on the state of the administration or to state opinions and answer questions" (Article 58).

These and other constitutional features regarding the legislature, coupled with the preponderant position of the President, were evidently designed to make the legislative branch amenable to presidential policies, particularly when the President's party had a comfortable majority in the National Assembly. This design is further emphasized by the fact that the President is vested with the veto power on legislative measures (Article 49) and that a two-thirds majority in the Assembly is necessary to override a veto.

The third major feature is the system of appointment of judges. In the Second Republic, an electoral body of judges elected the Chief Justice and justices of the Supreme Court, and the President merely confirmed such elections. In the Third Republic, the Chief Justice is appointed by the President with the consent of the National Assembly, upon the proposal of the Judicial Recommendation Council. Justices of the Supreme Court are also appointed by the President, upon the proposal of the Chief Justice, with the concurrence of the Judicial Recommendation Council. Lower-court judges are appointed by the Chief Justice through the decision of the Council of the Supreme Court Justices.

Presidential influence on the Judicial Recommendation Council is also considerable, since the nine-man council is composed of "four judges, two lawyers, one professor of law nominated by the President, the Minister of Justice and the Prosecutor General" (Article 99). The last three are nominated or appointed outright by the President. The tenure of the Chief Justice, which was ten years under both the Liberal and Democratic regimes, is now six years.

It is evident that the judicial branch, too, is made susceptible to the authority of the President, particularly when the President happens to be strong-willed. The Supreme Court of the Third Republic may make a "decision" to dissolve a political party, and the Supreme Court has the power to make the final review of the constitutionality of a law.

The fourth key feature is the constitutional provision for political parties. In the First and Second Republics, political parties found the legal basis for their rights indirectly through constitutional provisions for rights and duties of citizens, such as the freedom of speech and association. The amended or new constitution devotes Article 7 to political parties, and in this sense political parties enjoy an elevated constitutional status as long as their aims and activities are in keeping with "the basic democratic order."

The Constitution states that organization and activities of a political party "shall be democratic," and the fundamental law of the land "guarantees" a plural party system in the country. If the purposes or activities of a political party are contrary to the basic democratic order, however, "the Government shall begin an action against it in the Supreme Court for its dissolution and the political party shall be dissolved in accordance with the decision of the Supreme Court."

In another novel move, Article 36(3) makes nomination by a political party a prerequisite to candidacy in National Assembly elections, and Article 64(3) requires the same for a presidential candidate. Furthermore, an assemblyman forfeits his seat if he leaves or changes his party during his tenure, or when his party is dissolved (Article 38). This forfeiture stipulation does not apply in cases of "changes in party membership caused by amalgamation of parties or in case he has been expelled from his party."

It has been already noted that the head of the major opposition party in the National Assembly has been put on a government stipend, according to the Political Party Law based on the new Constitution. Political parties were also made tax-exempt. All of this exceptional attention was evidently intended to facilitate the organization of parties and, once organized, the stability of parties with representatives in the National Assembly. A common practice for many a politician in the past had been to run as an independent and then join the ruling party upon election or to switch from the opposition to the government party. The injunctions against the mobility of assemblymen were aimed at preventing recurrence of such phenomena. They were intended to decree a stability in party politics.

Another feature of the new constitution is that it elevates some procedural matters to the rank of constitutional stipulations while it restricts some substantive freedoms. Article 10 of the Constitution provides that no citizen shall be compelled to testify against himself in criminal cases and that, when a criminal defendant is unable to secure prompt assistance of counsel, the state shall assign a counsel. The same article also outlaws torture and sets limits to admissibility of a confession as evidence. These provisions formerly came under the criminal law, not the Constitution.

The first paragraph of Article 18 declares that all citizens shall enjoy freedom of speech and press and freedom of assembly and association. Other paragraphs of the same article, however, immediately place restrictions on these freedoms— restrictions that were not contained in old versions of the

Constitution. "Censorship in regard to motion pictures and dramatic plays" may be authorized for the maintenance of "public morality and social ethics." Presumably, "public morality and social ethics" were to be defined by the government or police authorities. The government may also prescribe "the standard for publication installations of a newspaper or press." Though this provision was justified in the minds of many who recalled past abuses of the freedom of the press, particularly in the Second Republic, the paragraph gave the government a potential weapon that might be used against publishers unfriendly to the government. Another paragraph of the article also stipulated that "the press or publication" shall not "infringe upon public morality and social ethics." The heyday of street demonstrations and outdoor political rallies formally came to an end as government "regulation" of outdoor assemblies became a constitutional principle.

In sum, the revised constitution has made the relative position of the President stronger than ever before, overshadowing the cabinet, legislative, and judicial branches. To this strong President is also given the emergency powers "necessary to maintain the public safety and order." When he decides that public safety and order are menaced, the President may mobilize the military forces or proclaim a state of siege of either an extraordinary or a precautionary stage. Under the state of siege, "special measures" may be taken with regard to "warrant system, freedom of speech, press, assembly and association, or with regard to the rights and powers of the Executive or the Judiciary" (Article 75). The freedom of the press, speech, and assembly, which may be substantially restricted constitutionally even without the declaration of the state of emergency, might be almost totally suspended under the state of siege.

The new constitution may be said to reflect the basic orientation of the members of the Supreme Council, the prime mover behind the new constitution. It constitutionalizes a strong presidential rule with readily available emergency powers particularly when the President controlled a majority in the National Assembly. The Constitution also embodies some "Spartan" ideas and opens avenues for regimentation in the name of "public morality and social ethics," while paying tribute to high-sounding democratic principles. The question of who would actually implement the constitutional provisions and set precedents under them became crucially important.

The Birth of the Third Republic

The presidential elections scheduled for October 15, 1963, were to be the tenth mass participation in electoral processes —including a constitutional referendum—since the May 10, 1948, general elections for the First National Assembly. Because the presidential elections were to mark formally the end of two and a half years of military rule, an overwhelming majority of Koreans showed intense interest in the campaigns as tens of thousands of citizens turned out to listen to candidates at mass rallies. The United States government had already given its official blessings to the elections so long as they were "free and fair" and indicated its willingness to honor the results. The United Nations Commission for the Unification and Rehabilitation of Korea (UNCURK) busily organized nine observation teams to be dispatched to all provinces during the elections.

The junta forces were ready for the elections with a presidential candidate whose image had been sharply and freshly etched on the minds of the electorate and a political party throbbing with youthful energy. The one group that was not ready for the showdown was the opposition candidates and their parties—divided, quarrelsome, meagerly funded, and often anachronistic in behavior. Even after the withdrawal of Hŏ Chŏng and Song Yo-ch'an from candidacy in the midst of the month-long campaign, there still remained five opposition presidential candidates against the single candidate of the Democratic Republican Party. The withdrawals of Hŏ and Song came only thirteen days and eight days respectively before the elections, contributing little to the unity of the opposition camp, although their withdrawals gave the elections an appearance of being a contest between Chung Hee Park and Yun Po-sŏn.

"Let's cast a ballot for the new worker and set him to work like an ox," declared the Democratic Republican Party, in a shrewd attempt to identify Park, with his humble origin in an impoverished farming village, with the population in agricultural regions of South Korea, who constituted about 70 per cent of the voters.[21] The campaign tactics suggested by the slogan were also designed to obscure the fact that Park was the powerful incumbent, or the Acting President, who already had been in a position to better their lives for about two and a half years. Park's regime had, indeed, tried to better the economic lot of farmers and fishermen by adopting many measures beneficial to them, including a "usurious loan clearance law." [22] As the Acting President, Park was able to time the ground-breaking ceremonies for over one hundred projects useful to the rural population in Kyŏngsang-namdo alone, largely a farming province, for September, 1963—the month before the presidential elections.

The opposition, though frustrated in their efforts to form a united front, based their hopes on the general hostility against a prolonged military rule and concentrated their efforts on arousing this hostility for the success of their separate campaigns to bring an end to military rule. This campaign strategy was essentially a negative one. The opposition groups appealed to voters to throw the junta forces out of power, but when the voters turned their eyes to the opposition groups they saw disgusting dogfights among "old politicians." The Committee for Joint Struggle against the Government, for instance, consisting of four opposition parties, only succeeded in coining a few campaign slogans to be used commonly by the four parties. Ironically, they wasted days seeking ways to discontinue scathing attacks on one another within the opposition camp.[23]

A notable phenomenon in the short and intensely heated campaign was the "ideological dispute." In a campaign speech, Park stated on September 23 that "these elections are an ideological contest between the hypocritical democracy [of the opposition] and the nationalistic democracy" of the junta forces and their supporters. Park flayed the opposition leaders as believers in tarnished democracy and toadyism. It was probably in reaction to this charge that Yun Po-sŏn stated on the following day that "there are in the government those who were involved in the rebellion in Yŏsu and Sunch'ŏn," the Communist-led military revolt of 1948. This accusation was an obvious attempt to revive and magnify a dead issue of some fifteen years before and to throw serious suspicion on Park's ideological orientation and about his suitability to be the President of South Korea. Yun further charged on October 9 that "the Democratic Republican Party was organized long before the elections owing to the political fund made available by the Communist party [of North Korea] and that Kim Chong-p'il had contacts with Hwang T'ae-sung," an influential member of the North Korean regime. The Civil Rule Party alleged that Hwang was a close friend of the deceased elder brother of General Park and that the Communist agent attempted to approach and influence Park.

Despite these attacks by his rival, however, Park refused to be drawn into the "ideological dispute" any further than denouncing these accusations as "unfounded charges." He concentrated his campaign program on the enunciation of "constructive policies and proposals." This strategy appeared to pay off by winning the sympathy of the people, who had become wary of mud-slinging campaigns. According to a commentator, "the opposition strategy was short-sighted and motivated by a McCarthyism that was rightly countered by the Democratic Republican Party." [24]

The outcome of the presidential race, however, was far from being a foregone conclusion. Despite the tangible and intangible advantages that the junta forces enjoyed, they had to overcome the widespread feeling that a "civilian" rule had to be restored. The race remained a seesaw game until the moment the results were announced. Out of 12,985,015 eligible voters, 11,036,175, or 84.99 per cent, participated in the presidential elections. The final returns of the voting are summarized in Table 5. A total of 954,977 votes, or about 8.65

Table 5. Results of the 1963 presidential elections

Candidate	Party	No. of votes	Percentage
Chung Hee Park	Democratic Republican Party	4,702,640	42.61
Yun Po-sŏn	Civil Rule Party	4,546,614	41.19
O Chae-yŏng	Autumn Wind Society	408,664	3.70
Pyŏn Yŏng-t'e	Justice of the People Party	224,443	2.03
Chang Yi-sŏk	Newly Emerging Party	198,837	1.80

Source: Compiled from Central Election Management Commission announcements.

per cent of the total ballots cast, were declared invalid. The reasons for invalidity included that 597,005 votes, or 5.41 per cent, were cast for Hŏ Chŏng and Song Yo-ch'an, both of whom had withdrawn their candidacies.

The difference between the winner and the runner-up was slim indeed, 156,026 votes, or a mere 1.42 per cent; while the total number of votes cast for the splinter candidates, including Hŏ and Song, who withdrew too late, was 1,428,949, or 12.94 per cent. If the opposition groups had united effectively under a pan-opposition candidate, instead of being senselessly and hopelessly divided, they could theoretically have mustered 54.13 per cent, against the 42.61 per cent of the winning general. Or if Hŏ and Song had withdrawn from the race early in the campaign, or if they had effectively persuaded their followers to switch their support to Yun Po-sŏn, Yun could have won by a comfortable margin. The "military rule," which every opposition candidate decried, would have been brought to an end.

Chung Hee Park, who had discarded his military uniform only a month and a half before the elections, was elected President, though a minority president. The United Nations Commission for the Unification and Rehabilitation of Korea, which sent observation teams into eight of the nine South Korean provinces, reported to the United Nations General Assembly that the presidential elections were held "in a free atmosphere and in an orderly, calm and proper manner." [25] Many Korean observers agreed with the findings of the Commission that the election was generally an honest contest with a minimum of irregularities. It should be added that this reflected credit on the military regime, which had administered the elections.

No sooner were the presidential elections over than South Koreans had to face the November 26 elections for national assemblymen, the eleventh general election since 1948. The tight presidential race prompted Park's supporters to redouble their efforts to capture the legislature, while the most obvious lesson of the presidential elections, the crying need for a united opposition against the junta-centered forces, was incredibly and completely lost among the opposition groups. The opposition politicians, who among themselves could not demonstrate the minimum degree of political sophistication, often appeared hopeful that the general electorate would miraculously exercise a keen political judgment and elect them, so that the legislature could restrain the powerful President. The political discipline within the efficiently managed Democratic Republican Party made it possible for it to nominate one carefully chosen candidate in each constituency and back him to the hilt. The opposition camp, on the other hand, had each of the four major parties running candidates in almost all districts, and there were seven minor opposition "parties" also running sizable numbers of candidates in many districts. The final registration figure showed a ratio of one candidate from the Democratic Republican Party to 6.4 candidates from the opposition camp,[26] dividing the antimilitary votes.

The four major opposition parties that were represented in the Committee for Joint Struggle against the Government again showed a preoccupation to attack one another rather than to coordinate their tactics against the progovernment party. The Civil Rule Party's "Strategy against Opposition Parties," uncovered by both the Democratic Party and the Party of the People, dramatically illustrated the extent of mistrust and antagonism among the opposition elements. "Let's put an end to the military rule," a slogan jointly adopted by the opposition, no longer had much substance or appeal to the electorate. After all, the opposition had already lost the presidential race, and it became clear that it was going to lose the parliamentary elections unless there was a mass withdrawal among the opposition candidates. There were 876 candidates from groups other than the Democratic Republican Party; only four withdrew.[27]

It was only three days before the November 26 elections that the news of President Kennedy's assassination reached Korea, to create "an abject void" [28] in the hearts of the Korean people. The Democratic Republican Party, which was far ahead of the opposition in its readiness for the voting, was quick to capitalize on the shocking occasion by announcing a twenty-four hour truce in campaigning. President-elect Park announced that he would attend the Kennedy funeral in Washington, and most news media now gave top priority to the coverage of the tragic event in the United States. The opposition's last-ditch attack on the progovernment party could find little outlet through news media. The sad news from the United States made an unexpected gap in the last-minute campaign schedule of the opposition, which needed every single day for campaigning. When election day came, only 69.8 per cent of the qualified voters cast their ballots. This was the lowest voter participation ever in Assembly elections; the depression syndrome triggered by the Kennedy assassination was evidently shared by the Korean nation. The unprecedentedly low turnout was definitely unfavorable to the opposition.

According to the National Assemblymen Election Law,[29] South Korea was divided into 131 single-member districts, and 44 additional seats, or one-third of the elected membership, were to be distributed in accordance with the proportion of votes received throughout South Korea by various parties. Article 125 of the law, which introduced the "nationwide district" system, or a version of proportional representation system, provided the formula for the distribution of the at-large seats among parties. The formula definitely favored a ruling party and other major parties in an attempt to stabilize party politics in the Assembly. The final result of the Assembly elections and of the proportional distribution of the seats according to the formula, according to an announcement by the Central Election Management Commission on November 30, 1963, is given in Table 6.

Table 6. Results of the 1963 Assembly elections (by party)

Party	Elected	At large	Total
Democratic Republican Party	88	22	110
Civil Rule Party	27	14	41
Democratic Party	8	5	13
Liberal Democratic Party	6	3	9
Party of the People	2	0	2
Total	131	44	175

Source: Republic of Korea, Central Election Management Commission, *Yŏkde kukhoe ŭiwŏn sŏnkŏ sanghang* (The Patterns of Successive National Assembly Elections), 1967.

The Democratic Republican Party won an impressive number of seats, just seven seats short of the two-thirds majority of 117 seats; while the Civil Rule Party of Yun Po-sŏn won merely 41 seats. The three splinter parties together won a total of only 24 seats. Even in the unlikely event of complete unity among the four opposition parties in the Assembly, their total strength would be 65 votes, barely over one-third of the total. The seven minor parties, which also ran over two hundred candidates, failed to win a single seat. The most notable fact was that the Democratic Republican Party occupied 62.9 per cent of the Assembly seats with only 33.5 per cent support of the voters, because it had won the largest single block of votes and because of the proportional representation formula. The opposition held only 37.1 per cent of the seats with 66.5 per cent support of the voters, because of the formula and particularly because of their divisions.

Despite all the handicaps that shackled the opposition groups under the Supreme Council, the percentage figures showed that they could still have won both the presidential race and the Assembly elections—if only they had learned the value of political discipline and sophistication. That they had not learned this lesson brought common ruin for them all; in fact, they proved even less astute politically than the Korean masses.

It was hardly surprising that thirty Assembly members were former military officers who had been key figures of the military revolution; twenty-eight of them belonged to the Democratic Republican Party and two to the opposition.[30] In a 175-seat Assembly divided by many party and factional lines, a group of thirty retired officers of the armed forces gave a definite militaristic coloration to the entire Assembly, as long as the officers could remain cohesive. This bloc appears even more significant when considered in the light of the fact that 71 per cent of the Democratic Republican Party members in the Assembly were from thirty to forty-nine years old, an age bracket to which which most of the retired officers belonged. In a country where age still remains a factor in understanding behavioral patterns, it meant that the group of former officers could speak a common language with a large majority of the ruling party members. Most opposition members, on the other hand, were from forty to fifty-nine years old.

The third revolutionary pledge had read, in part: "We shall inculcate fresh and wholesome moral and mental attitudes among the people." At least in the sense that younger blood was transfused into the parliamentary body of the republic, a part of this pledge appeared fulfilled. How the legislative organ would react to the different—militaristic—

type of blood remained to be seen. Bringing about a "shift of generation" of the political elite in Korea was one of the professed political goals of the military regime. That 108 out of 175 Assembly members were newcomers to the legislature, or that only 38.2 per cent of the membership were re-elected to the legislature, meant that a substantial shift actually occurred at least among the legislators. The turnover rates in the Korean legislature had always been considerable, but never this high. All these features, taken together, suggested that a new breed of men—younger, tougher, less experienced, but more regimented—was to dominate the Sixth Assembly of Korea. It was certainly going to be compatible with General-turned-President Park.

The Third Republic of Korea was officially born on December 17, 1963, when Chung Hee Park was inaugurated President and the Sixth National Assembly convened amidst pomp and flummeries. Park, at forty-six, was the youngest Korean President ever elected. The youthful President vowed to free the nation "from century-old yokes" and to "reform the nation with sweat, blood, and work." The rule by the Supreme Council for National Reconstruction officially came to an end, as the chairman of that junta became the President of the Third Republic.

Postscript

It is probably premature at present, when President Park's first term is barely over and his second is just beginning, to evaluate the performance of the Park administration. An abundance of claims and counter-claims have been made concerning the achievements, or lack of them, of the Park government. It will be necessary and more fruitful to distill these claims in the future, when more authenticated records are available and when a better perspective for evaluation is attainable. This postscript will be limited, therefore, to a discussion and analysis of the presidential elections of May 3 and the National Assembly elections of June 8, 1967. Some tentative remarks about the regime's functions will be necessary, nevertheless, as they are pertinent to this postscript.

On February 2, 1967, President Park accepted the unanimous nomination of his ruling Democratic Republican Party to run for a second—and constitutionally his last—four-year term. The nomination was proposed by Kim Chong-p'il, the influential party chairman who has remained a key political figure ever since the 1961 coup. President Park told a party convention that he had decided to seek re-election because he could not give up in the middle of his effort to "modernize our fatherland." The "national modernization" of South Korea has been one of the most emphasized policy objectives of the Park administration, leading a commentator to observe that Korean politics has reached a stage where the legitimacy of a regime is based on—instead of a democratic mandate—the ability to promote "national interest" as officially interpreted to mean "national modernization." [1]

While the well-organized and well-financed ruling party nominated the single best-known candidate, the opposition camp was still badly split among several aspirants until the very end of January. A series of "meetings of four leaders" in the opposition camp, aimed at nominating a pan-opposition candidate, appeared to be bogged down. The endeavor was then led by Yun Po-sŏn, presidential candidate of the Shinhandang, or New Korea Party, and Yu Chin-o, presidential candidate of the Minjungdang, or Masses Party.[2] Observers recalled the 1963 contest between the military-led and solidly unified Democratic Republican forces and the hopelessly divided opposition groups, and some predicted a repeat performance of the same pattern. The major opposition leaders "surprised almost everyone" [3] in South Korea when on February 5 they were successful in uniting the main rival factions and agreeing on Yun Po-sŏn as the standard bearer of the Shinmindang, or New Democratic Party, to be formed by the merger of Shinhandang and the Minjungdang. Yu Chin-o withdrew from the presidential race and became chairman of the newly merged party, which was formally launched on February 7. The merger was called a political miracle by opposition figures and the principal leaders of the New Democratic Party attempted to infuse confidence and enthusiasm among their followers by publicly discussing possibilities of the "transfer of the government" to them through election victories. Many recalled that Park had defeated Yun by a razor-thin margin of 156,000 votes in 1963, when the opposition was completely divided.

It remained to be seen, however, if the activities of the new organization would in fact become coordinated and integrated, and if the two groups could transcend factional and hegemonic considerations within what was dubbed a pan-opposition organization. Could the merger at the top and central levels insure meaningful intermeshing at the lower district level, particularly when the merged organization had to nominate a single candidate per district in the Assembly elections? Was the merger in February soon enough for the spring elections? It certainly failed to create a "pan-opposition" movement; when the registration period closed on April 3, there were still six opposition presidential candidates [4] running against General Park. Even after Sŏ Min-ho withdrew his candidacy on April 28, there remained four minor candidates who had no chance of winning the presidency but who were certainly likely to siphon off opposition votes.

The candidates started stumping around the country, and huge crowds were mobilized by the ruling party and Yun's camp. When Park addressed the first massive campaign rally on April 17 in Taejŏn, about 100,000 heard him characterize his administration and ruling party as the only force capable of attaining the modernization of South Korea. When Yun accused the Park government of fostering "four big evils" —"dictatorship, corruption, abuse of special privileges, and subservience" [5] of the people to the ruling authorities—about 70,000 avidly listened to him in Pusan. The massive turnout of potential voters at the campaign rallies of Park and Yun demonstrated the ability of both the Democratic Republican Party and the New Democratic Party to reach out effectively to voters and, possibly, a high degree of politicization of the qualified voters themselves. That voters virtually ignored other, lesser candidates' campaign speeches and promises once again indicated, as in 1963, that the Korean masses were politically more astute than some presidential hopefuls who were running without any conceivable hope of winning.

A second encouraging aspect that emerged from the campaigning was that the major contenders' public pronouncements were more issue-oriented than in 1963. Policy matters were more frequently debated, and there were more meaningful exchanges between the major contenders on such substantive issues as economic policies and the rate of economic growth, Korean involvement in the Vietnamese War, and various approaches to the modernization of South Korea. The speeches of Park and Yun were remarkably free of overt attempts at character assassination, though their examples were not always followed at lower levels. On the other hand, they again displayed the familiar tendency to make excessive campaign promises that were bound to prove empty words.

The principal differences between the two major contending parties in terms of their policy lines, claims, and advocacies could be summed up as follows: [6]

Domestic Politics

Democratic Republican Party: Promote closer cooperation among political parties for the betterment of the political atmosphere. Assure fair elections and guarantee the political neutrality of government employees. Punish violators of election laws, regardless of their party affiliations. Promote the early realization of of two-party politics. Accomplish the "modernization of the fatherland"—the principal objective of the Democratic Republican Party, a "working party." Oppose the political utilization of police forces. Strengthen the financial bases for local governmental units and establish local legislative units that could be compatible with Korean realities. Delegate to local governments a substantial number of administrative responsibilities in meeting people's needs, including licensing.

New Democratic Party: Replant the roots of democracy that

the Park regime disrupted. Amend the Constitution to resurrect the State Affairs Council (cabinet) as a decision-making body instead of a consultative organ, to enable the National Assembly to resolve nonconfidence of cabinet members, and to abolish reelection of the President. Guarantee the freedoms of speech, press, assembly, and association as long as the enjoyment of such freedoms is not intended to destroy the democratic order. Abolish the Central Intelligence Agency, or restrict its activities to purely anti-Communist surveillance. Nullify the Political Party Law, and improve election laws. Promote early realization of local autonomy. Eliminate all undemocratic practices by government officials.

Foreign Relations and National Defense

Democratic Republican Party: Strengthen friendly relations with the free world and neutralist states. Promote regional unity among Asian and Pacific nations. Promote economic cooperation with free, friendly states. Promote diplomatic cooperation with Japan on the basis of equality and friendship. Improve protective measures for Korean residents in Japan. Supply more modern equipment to the armed forces and strengthen the national defense position. Improve the payment and diet for military personnel. Continue the active participation in the Vietnamese War, at the time employing about 46,000 Korean troops, and equip the troops with up-to-date "automatic weapons." Establish a "Free Asian University" in Seoul.

New Democratic Party: Maintain a strong defense posture for the protection of the national territory, and practice effective and selective diplomacy. Establish "free" diplomatic relations with Japan. Oppose any further Korean troop dispatches to Vietnam, in order not to weaken defensive strength in Korea. Improve treatment of those troops already in Vietnam. Strengthen the Korean position vis-à-vis the United States regarding Korean national security. Practice effective trade diplomacy. Stop increasing the number of ineffectual diplomatic establishments abroad. Guarantee the political neutrality of the armed forces. Formalize a systematic personnel policy for the military and improve the treatment of military personnel.

Economy

Democratic Republican Party: Recognize that the First Five-Year Plan was a spectacular success. Assert that the average annual gain of 8.5 per cent in gross national product was far higher than any other Asian state, and the 11.9 per cent gain in 1966 was the highest in the world. Attain 8.5 per cent annual growth under the Second Five-Year Plan. Contain the price increase at a level lower than 7 per cent annually. Promote creation of over 2 million jobs. Expand the exportation of Korean manpower. Raise government employees' salaries by 30 per cent annually. Decrease the fertilizer price. Increase foodstuff production by 40 per cent and attain self-sufficiency in food supply. Establish a system of governmental subsidies for agricultural losses due to natural calamities and decrease the tax rate for farming families. Promote modernization of fishing industries. Establish technical assistance and consultation centers for medium and small businesses.

New Democratic Party: Promote the economic welfare of the masses, instead of the enrichment of a privileged few. Curb capital investments in the interest of the privileged groups. Curb the heavy emphasis on industry and place equal emphasis on both industry and agriculture. Decrease the fertilizer price. Establish a price control board. Curb indirect taxes and place emphasis on direct taxes. Increase inheritance tax rates and decrease other tax rates. Increase exportation of manufactured goods using domestic raw materials. Correct the unfavorable balance of trade with Japan. Promote modernization of business management.

These major issues were extensively debated during the presidential campaign. On the day of the presidential elections, May 3, fine weather prevailed throughout the country. Exactly 7,863 polling places opened early in the morning, awaiting 13,935,093 qualified voters. On May 6, the Central Election Management Commission officially announced the

final returns of the balloting, in which 83.6 per cent of qualified voters participated (see Table 7).

Table 7. Results of the 1967 presidential elections

Candidate	Party	No. of votes	Percentage
Chung Hee Park	Democratic Republican Party	5,688,666	48.84
Yun Po-sŏn	New Democratic Party	4,526,541	38.97
O Chae-yŏng	Korean Unification Party	264,533	2.27
Kim Chun-yŏn	Masses Party	245,368	2.13
Chŏn Chin-han	Korean Independence Party	232,180	1.99
Yi Se-jin	Justice Party	98,433	0.85

Source: Compiled from Central Election Management Commission
announcements.

Park's winning margin over Yun of 1,162,125 votes was of
landslide proportions when compared with his margin of
156,026 votes over the same opponent in 1963. Whereas in
1963 the opposition candidates together had mustered a total
of 54.13 per cent of valid votes against 42.61 per cent for the
winning general, the opposition candidates together polled
46.21 per cent against Park's 48.84 per cent in 1967. It appears
that even if there had been a single opposition candidate in
1967, Park would not have been dislodged. The popular base
of the Park regime was significantly expanded.

According to expenditure reports submitted to the Central
Election Management Commission, the Democratic Republican Party spent 243,170,851 *won* for the presidential campaigns, and the New Democratic Party expended less than
one-tenth of that amount, or 22,762,356 *won*. What the splinter parties spent was a mere pittance, with the Masses Party
reporting the third largest amount—approximately one one-

hundredth of that reported by the Democratic Republican Party.[7] Such discrepancies led, predictably, to opposition charges that the affluent ruling party, having developed intricate ties with the industrial and business world, had "bought" numerous votes. In terms of the amount reported by the Democratic Republican Party, however, only about 6 won, or the equivalent of about two U.S. cents, were spent for each valid vote cast for President Park.

Most observers agreed that the presidential elections were largely free and fair. The apparent absence of tension in the elections was hailed as suggesting a new maturity in Korean politics. Most instances of election irregularities reported during the polling appeared to be minor. The polling was conducted under the inspection of the United Nations Commission for Unification and Rehabilitation of Korea, a seven-nation body that is supposed to inform the General Assembly of Korean political progress.[8] The *Japan Times* editorialized that the Park "regime is firmly built on a democratic basis," [9] and the *New York Times* exclaimed that "the democratic process had obviously taken hold" throughout South Korea and that "a costly American investment in Asian democracy seemed to be paying off." [10]

Park's clear-cut victory might be attributable to a number of major developments in his first term. Among the more important was that the Korean people evidently valued the high degree of internal political stability and order that the Park government created and maintained. The regime was also capable of projecting the image of Park as a hard-working and effective leader building momentum for the modernization and industrialization of South Korea. Park had been kept constantly in the limelight through his many state visits to friendly nations, return visits by foreign chiefs of states, the dispatch of Korean troops to Vietnam, the hosting of many international conferences, and frequent visits to various parts of the country inspecting "modernization projects." Kim Chong-p'il declared that Park's overwhelming victory reflected a "reconfirmation by the people of a hard-working and building President."

An equally, or even more important, factor that contributed to Park's victory was that a "dramatic economic growth has taken place since 1963." [11] According to figures announced by the government-directed Bank of Korea, the annual average growth rate for the three years between 1963 and 1965 was 8.8 per cent. [12] According to another recent report, the gross national product rose a staggering 11.9 per cent in 1966. [13] During the execution of the First Five-Year Plan, extremely favorable conditions for South Korea's economic development have prevailed—among them, Korean participation in the Vietnamese conflict, which has brought special procurement orders and contracts to Korea and sizable incomes for a large number of Korean technicians, engineers, and troops in Vietnam. These economic lifts, combined with internal stability, led to what the administration acclaimed as a spectacularly successful First Five-Year Plan.

The beneficial impact of this development was directly felt and visible in industrial and urban centers, and this fact was reflected in the heavy support given in such areas to Park, who was personally identified with the development. Often, in past elections, there had been a discernible pattern of opposition parties' receiving support from relatively sophisticated urban centers and the ruling party's being supported by voters in politically less astute rural areas. In 1963, for instance, out of approximately 3,210,000 valid votes cast in urban centers, Park received only 37.8 per cent and Yun 57.1 per cent, while out of about 6,870,000 valid rural ballots, 50.8 per cent supported Park and 39.5 per cent went to Yun.

In the 1967 presidential elections, however, out of approximately 3,550,000 valid votes cast in urban centers, 50.4 per cent supported Park and 37.7 per cent were for Yun. About 52.2 per cent of the approximately 7,420,000 valid rural votes supported Park, and 42.4 per cent voted for Yun. Though it was thus true that Park defeated the opposition in rural areas, he also led in twenty-two out of thirty-three cities.[14]

The overall political and economic situation, therefore, held out the attraction of four more years of stability and growth —if the Park regime could secure a working majority in the National Assembly through free and fair elections. Buoyed by his overwhelming victory, President Park urged the electorate to give him a stable majority in the legislature to enable him to carry out his pledge to accomplish South Korea's economic development and complete the Second Five-Year Plan. The plan had already been initiated in January, 1967, a year and a half ahead of the original schedule. The opposition New Democratic Party, which held 60 out of 175 seats in the outgoing assembly, did its utmost to allay its crushing defeat in the presidential elections by an appeal to the voters: "Give us a majority in the Assembly so as to check the autocratic rule of the President." This situation was reminiscent of the comparable stage in the 1963 elections.

On March 13, the well-organized Democratic Republican Party was already able to announce the party-endorsed candidates—one for each of the 131 election districts—for the June 8 elections. When the registration for the Assembly elections closed on May 15, there were 702 candidates representing eleven parties running for the 131 seats to be popularly and directly elected, and there were 119 nominees of the parties for the "all-nation-district" or proportional representation seats to be apportioned on the basis of the popular votes each party received.[15] Once again, the opposition groups had an average of more than four men running against the single ruling party candidate in each district, though few voters now seemed to take the splinter groups seriously.

Whereas the presidential campaigns had been carried out in a generally dignified atmosphere, electioneering for the Assembly quickly appeared to turn into a free-for-all. The ruling party candidates tended to be overly aggressive and the opposition groups apparently entered the arena with a feeling of desperation. Many local organizations of the Democratic Republican Party were said to have used every means at their disposal to mobilize, influence, and capture, or "procure," votes. Newspapers ran pictures of tipsy women singing and dancing at a campaign rally, while an evidently drunken woman collapsed and slept on a straw mat nearby. A Korean paper also ran pictures of men alleged to be ruling party organizers passing cash to potential voters. The Democratic Republican Party apparently had abundant campaign funds, while the opposition groups had extremely limited budgets. The major opposition group, the New Democratic Party, charged that the government was illegally and unreasonably suppressing opposition campaign activities, and the National Police Director announced that the police were alerted throughout South Korea as tension rose dangerously. He declared that the police alert was aimed at correcting a "degenerated election atmosphere."

Yu Chin-o, chairman of the New Democratic Party, charged that the "June 8 elections will turn out to be an unprecedentedly rigged balloting, worse than any other irregularities in the past." Yu, the most prominent opposition leader since Yun's defeat in the presidential race, then darkly indicated that the opposition members elected to the Assembly through such unfair contests might refuse to register and be duly seated.[16] This statement, issued two days before the elections, was the first public indication that the opposition might boycott the new Assembly.

When the balloting was completed on June 8, the Central Election Management Commission announced that 11,202,313 out of 14,717,354 qualified voters, or only 76.1 per cent, had participated in the elections,[17] one of the lowest participation rates in any South Korean election and markedly lower than the 83.6 per cent that had voted in the presidential elections a month before. The New Democratic Party quickly denounced the June elections as the "most viciously rigged in the history of our country," even worse than the scandalous voting of March 15, 1960, that had led to the Student Uprising and the downfall of the late President Syngman Rhee. Foreign observers, who presumably had little partisan interest in the outcome, reported that "widespread violence and irregularities at the polls marred" the Assembly elections and referred to "numerous cases of vote-buying and 'proxy voting' by Government supporters in many areas" and to "a dozen incidents in which opposition poll watchers were beaten and driven out of polling stations when they protested irregularities." [18]

The election results officially announced by the Central Election Management Commission showed a lopsided victory by the ruling party. The Democratic Republican Party had won 102 out of 131 district seats, which entitled it to 27 out of 44 proportional seats. The ruling party thus occupied 129 out of the total of 175 seats in the Assembly—12 seats more than a two-thirds majority of 117, or 19 more than its strength in the outgoing Assembly. The New Democratic Party had elected 28, and 17 proportional seats, bringing their total to a mere 45. The only minor party candidate elected was Sŏ

Min-ho. No national proportional representation seats were awarded to any of the nine splinter parties, as none of them had won the minimum of three seats required.

Despite President Park's pledge that there would be "no constitutional amendments to allow prolongation of the two-term tenure of the President" [19] even if the ruling party won a two-thirds majority, many were gravely concerned about just such a possibility. The New Democratic Party declared that the June 8 elections were a "second *coup d'état*" led by Park, and demanded that the entire congressional election results be declared null and void. Defying a strict government ban, thousands of university and high school students once again took to the streets to demand new congressional elections. The government authorities closed down scores of colleges and universities and well over a hundred high schools in various parts of the country for an indefinite period. Helmeted, club-swinging riot police charged into the demonstrating students, who fought back with barrages of rocks.

The forty-four members of the New Democratic Party who had been elected to the Assembly formally resolved by June 15 to boycott the proceedings of the new legislature unless the government called new elections and punished those responsible for "*coup d'état*-like election rigging." This was an extremely serious action. Article 7 (1) of the Constitution "guaranteed" a "plural party system" in Korean politics and, by implication, in the National Assembly. The constitutional provision was "to prevent dictatorship by one party." [20] The National Assembly rules stipulated that there must exist more than one "parliamentary negotiation body," the organization of elected assemblymen belonging to a party, for the Assembly to function legally. The minimum number required for a parliamentary negotiation body was ten elected and duly seated members. The Assembly rule also required that standing committees be formed by members of more than one party. Article 38 of the Constitution also provided that an assemblyman forfeits his seat "when he leaves or changes his party" during his tenure, though this provision was not to apply in cases of "changes in party membership caused by amalgamation of parties or in case he has been expelled from his party."

As there was only one assemblyman elected from a third party, the Assembly now appeared paralyzed as long as the elected members of the New Democratic Party remained unified in their refusal to register with the Assembly and be duly seated. President Park issued a special statement on June 16 admitting that election rigging and irregularities had been uncovered by investigating authorities in certain districts. He declared, however, that these were only localized incidents and not a general phenomenon. The President announced that he had directed the "expulsion" of eight elected assemblymen from the Democratic Republican Party pending further investigations. Police arrested two of these assemblymen, scores of campaign workers of both the ruling party and the opposition groups, and local government officials. The ruling party also expelled 125 party officials, evidently in an attempt to placate the opposition and the demonstrating students, of whom 525 were arrested in Seoul alone.[21] Still, about five thousand opposition party members and other citizens continued to stage riotous demonstrations in downtown Seoul, now demanding that President Park resign. Police whisked away Yu Chin-o, the New Democratic Party chairman, and other notable opposition leaders, fired tear grenades, and again charged into the rioting crowd.

Three influential nonpolitical organizations also expressed grave concern over alleged irregularities.[22] The usually progovernment Korean Businessmen's Association called on the government to "assume moral responsibility for irregularities" and to hold new elections in those constituencies where frauds had been discovered. The Korean Christian Federation, with 3,500,000 members, also charged that the election irregularities had resulted from the "abuse of government power and lack of sincerity to practice democracy." The Korean Bar Association declared that government officials from the Premier down to local police chiefs had staged "an all-out illegal campaign" to support ruling party candidates during the elections.

By the July 8 deadline for filing law suits arising from election disputes, there were an astounding 266 cases formally registered with the courts—in sharp contrast with the 37 cases filed after the 1963 elections. Many of the 266 suits asserted that members of the ruling party had violated election regulations, and contested the validity of the election of these ruling party members.[23]

Mass communication media had reported favorably on the integrity of the Park administration during and after the presidential elections. They were plainly disenchanted, however, with the administration's handling of the congressional elections and the aftermath, as exemplified by the lengthy "special features" of the influential opinion journal *Shindonga*, which highlighted the theme of "Contesting the Rigged Elections."[24] Foreign presses, which had also been impressed with the fairness of the presidential elections, now severely criticized the Park regime. The *New York Times*, for instance, editorialized that while Park's own election was "sufficiently honest" the June 8 elections were "so crooked that Washington has not yet got over a sense of embarrassment."[25] The *Washington Post* condemned "government harassment of the opposition" during the elections, and declared that the Park government "is essentially a military regime backed by the United States."[26]

In this unsettled atmosphere, the forty-nine-year-old soldier-statesman took the presidential oath of office on July 1 to begin a second four-year term. He vowed to fight the country's three enemies—"poverty, corruption, and communism" [27]—and coupled this vow with an appeal to South Koreans to "regain our reason and presence of mind," an apparent reference to the demonstrations, riots, and hunger strikes touched off by charges of election rigging. In his inaugural address, the President acknowledged that "unlawful acts" had been perpetrated in the Assembly elections. He rejected, however, demands by the enraged opposition that the election results be nullified and promised court action against the culprits. "One who has violated a law will be punished by the law," he declared. "Errors committed in the process of democratization will be mended in accordance with democratic means."

Even while the President was making his inaugural speech, accusations that Park's party had won by fraud could be heard from a loudspeaker on the roof of the New Democratic Party headquarters, some three hundred yards away from the inauguration site. Some fifteen hundred university students clashed again with riot police on the eve of the inaugural, and eighty leaders of the New Democratic Party were reported to be on a hunger strike in the opposition party headquarters, where there was a brief scuffle when policemen attempted unsuccessfully to enter the building and seize the loudspeaker. Riotous student demonstrations in Seoul resumed on July 3 with the reopening of the universities for the examinations that conclude the spring term—indicating that public resentment of the way the Assembly elections had been conducted ran deep.[28]

The Seventh National Assembly was also formally inaugurated on July 10 for a four-year term with all the ruling party members in attendance, and amid continued opposition protests. The 44 members of the New Democratic Party and the one splinter party member were absent. Approximately thirty opposition assemblymen-elect and thirty other opposition party members staged a sitdown on the front steps of the Assembly building, shouting such slogans as "One-party legislature is illegal!" and "We want new elections!" Thus formalized was the opposition boycott of the new Assembly, which could paralyze the new legislature on constitutional grounds and on the basis of Assembly rules.

Chairman Yu Chin-o of the New Democratic Party, the principal drafter of the original Constitution of the Korean Republic, charged that the ruling party had prejudiced the nation's constitutional government by opening the Assembly unlawfully. In a message sent to the Assembly, President Park deplored the opposition boycott and stressed that problems resulting from election irregularities should be dealt with by the legislature and by court procedures.

A bitterly uncompromising deadlock thus forecast a prolonged period of political unrest. Significantly, however, it is a contest that is fought, partially at least, over problems that arise in connection with democratic institutions and practices. The final resolution of this crisis will significantly affect the future verdict in the continuing trial of democracy in Korea.

Conclusion

The government of the Republic of Korea was inaugurated in 1948 in the southern half of the divided peninsula under the aegis of the United States government, which was eager to terminate the costly and thankless task of ruling through a military government a "liberated" people of South Korea. While a firm Communist control was being established in the Soviet-occupied north, the political leaders in the American zone had been becoming impatient to attain independent statehood for South Korea. The first general elections in Korea were supervised by United Nations teams, a "democratic" constitution was hurriedly adopted by the new National Assembly, and the very first representative government was launched in a Korea that was re-emerging from the Japanese colonial domination that had terminated an indigenous dynastic rule in 1910.

The legal-institutional superstructure of the new Republic suddenly appeared democratic and modern. The political substructure or culture, however, had been long accustomed to debilitating authoritarian rule. Thus the governmental systems were not founded on the existing political realities of South Korea; in fact, there existed a huge gap between the idealistic aspirations and the realistic capabilities of the new political system. Such incongruity and disparity—possibly a real villain in Korean politics—was to cause tensions and disturbances rather than harmony and stability.

While some members of the new political elite proudly parroted almost flawless democratic jargon, their deeds revealed a wide discrepancy between their formal pronouncements and their concrete deeds. The Korean masses were confused and often enraged with the new, inexperienced, and inconsistent leaders. It also became apparent that the new or "borrowed" constitution often lacked political, cultural, and socio-economic content or applicability to Korean realities. The new fundamental law of the land, therefore, tended to become a mere "decorative document." The country began to suffer from schizophrenia.

Under the circumstances, the role of recognized leaders was to be crucial in motivating and encouraging the nation to function in a manner generally consonant with democratic principles and processes. An unchallengeable position of one-man leadership was won by President Rhee, especially after the assassination of Kim Ku. From the beginning, awesome personalism triumphed over institutionalism in the Rhee administration. Although the constitution proclaimed at least the traditional three-way separation of powers, this was quickly made a fiction.

Understandably, there was an acute shortage of trained manpower in every field in newly independent Korea, particularly in governmental bureaucracy or political organizations. This shortage was aggravated, first, by the suspicion and hostility that marred relations between hyper-nationalistic political leaders and officials and politicians who had served the Japanese colonial regime. Secondly, the shortage was further complicated by the almost pathological suspicion and enmity that Rhee and his anti-Communist followers showed toward liberals and left-leaning intellectuals. These facts severely limited the ground from which Korea could recruit its manpower, and that grouping tended to be extreme rightist and conservative.

On this base, Rhee's autocracy was firmly established as early as July, 1952, as a consequence of the "political crisis" in the wartime capital. The elected representatives of the Korean people, the assemblymen, yielded to Rhee at every turn. In applying political pressure to any group that opposed his rule, the existence of the Communist regime in the North and the tension attributed to this situation provided Rhee and his apologists handy cover for usurpation of the powers of the legislature.

In this sense, Communism not only constituted a visible, external, physical threat to "democracy" in South Korea, but also accelerated the formation of an extreme rightist autocracy within a country that was supposedly "democratic." Loud protestations of anti-Communism had rallied the conservative coalition in the late 1940's, and by 1952, Rhee was supreme under the "twin watchwords of internal stability and militant anti-communism." [1] Tragic rebellions in South Korea and, particularly, the Korean War tended to give the above watchwords certain substance. When the question of national survival was at stake, few in Korea dared demand democratic and constitutional rights or procedures.

Once Rhee's overlordship was attained, the political party that he created also became supreme. Many "parties" that crowded the Korean political scene were either factions or groups of factions. Many of them were built around a leader or group of leaders, and they disappeared with them, leaving behind disturbing influences upon the growth of democratic party politics. These parties were often the hotbeds of intrigue, corruption, and violence. Nothing has discredited "democracy" more in the eyes of the Korean masses, or has made them more cynical about politics, than this scandalous politicking.

The Second Republic under President Yun and Premier Chang, inaugurated as a consequence of the violent Student Uprising, had greater inclinations and promises of practicing democracy than had the First Republic. The factional deadlock in the legislature of the Second Republic, however, meant executive impotence in a country with a crying need for bold executive action. Since the parliamentary system of the Second Republic made the executive dependent on a majority in the legislature, most governmental activities became paralyzed when the Assembly was divided into feuding and warring factions. It was a scene of political chaos. This situation was to give rise to voices seeking a paradoxical "partyless democracy." These voices were only one logical step removed from demands for a strong-man rule.

In the first thirteen years of the "republican" era in Korea, periodic elections were often farcical, costly, and bloody rituals. It proved relatively easy to march the docile people to the polls. But these exercises of fundamental rights of citizens were too often manipulated to install an autocrat or his coteries. As elections became fictions, designed to give the appearance of legitimacy to ruling groups, the elections lost meaning to the majority of the masses. To a significant degree, therefore, the concepts of democracy also lost meaning.

While these undemocratic and antidemocratic practices were being repeated in Korea, tenacious attempts were made to create and maintain the myth of Korea's being a "democratic" state. Rhee himself habitually talked about Korea's being the "bulwark of democracy in the east," and some hopeful foreign observers praised the "promising experiment in democracy" in Korea. The United States government had fairly consistently encouraged the democratization of Korea, as indicated by the official positions of Truman, Acheson, Herter, Magruder, and Green. In any case, the Korean people were repeatedly told by opinion molders that their country was "democratic," whereas democracy in its proper sense had not existed in Korea. For those Koreans who believed this myth to be democracy, the concept became disreputable even before they had a real chance to experience democracy. A political myth is often costly and destructive; the democratic myth in Korea was no exception.

The *coup d'état* of May, 1961, was the most drastic turning point in the painfully turbulent trial of democracy in Korea. It violently liquidated the crises of authority and consequent immobilism of the Second Republic, which had been unable to provide effective political leadership and efficient administration within the institutional framework of a democratic government. Following the coup, the revolutionary soldiers established a highly centralized, tightly regimented, almost omnipotent military regime under the leadership of General Chung Hee Park. The democratic polity—at least in terms of theory—of the Second Republic was discredited and discarded. The representative superstructure was decreed out of existence, as were most freedoms. While the military regime, which, by definition, could not be democratic, was being born, statements issued by the two top American representatives in Korea, General Magruder and Minister Green, were the only voices heard in defense of a "freely elected" or "democratic" government in South Korea.

No Koreans attempted in any effective way to resurrect "democracy" as practiced in the Second Republic. Nor was this possible in a Korea ruled by martial law for a year and a half following the coup. Most Koreans were disillusioned with an impotent and chaotic "democratic" republic in which a bankrupt economy threatened the livelihood of the over-whelming majority of the people; they placidly accepted the military regime.

The Supreme Council for National Reconstruction launched a dizzying flurry of activities, most of which were immedi-ately visible and spectacular, if not prudently planned and always far-reaching. A whole generation of "old politicians" were blacklisted, demoralized, and "purged" in effect. The military junta earnestly and impatiently attempted to trigger dramatic economic growth. An economic miracle in Korea, however, could not be created out of thin air by military decrees. For the vast majority of people, economic despair continued to exist, amid whispers of brazen corruption among the new ruling group. Some Koreans now ruefully recalled Lord Acton's dictum: "Power tends to corrupt, and absolute power corrupts absolutely."

The constitutional "amendments" engineered by the mili-tary regime produced a virtually new constitution. It has made the position of the President supreme, eliminating the possibility of executive-legislative rivalry and deadlock. It might be said that the gap between the governmental systems and existing political culture was definitely and realistically narrowed. The governmental system as a whole was made more viable and functional in the Korean environment.

The "old politicians," perennially divided and bickering among themselves, were powerless to prevent the far-reaching political transformation or General Park's ascension to the presidency. Park's new vehicle was the Democratic Republi-can Party, methodically organized by the youthful force that had executed the military coup, and its new allies. Thus began the "civilian" government of the Third Republic, with the promises of political stability.

Meanwhile the Korean masses have begun to show a remarkable degree of political sophistication. The results of the 1956 elections that forced Rhee to accept Chang as his Vice-President and the 1963 elections in which the margin of General Park's victory was slim indeed may be indications that the Korean people are becoming politically mature. When these elections were relatively fair and free, the anonymous and seemingly acquiescent Korean masses exercised keen collective judgment that stunned many politicians. In fact, in the 1963 and 1967 elections the Korean people were politically more astute than those undisciplined politicians who belonged to numerous myopic and quarrelsome factions. Ultimately, democracy in Korea will depend upon such political developments among the people themselves.

It is probable that the democratic superstructure, or at least its façade that the Korean nation had maintained for nearly two decades, and certain practices and processes such as the general elections in which the Koreans participated eleven times in one form or another, have left certain lasting influences on the political culture of the Korean nation. The educational system that taught democratic principles, theories, and values to a new generation of young Koreans also might have left indelible imprints on the minds of those students, who have experienced and possibly contemplated the results of the Student Uprising that toppled what appeared to be an impregnable regime.

Now that the Koreans have lost many of their democratic freedoms, or at least the constitutional and legal bases for them, numerous Koreans are giving indications that they are suddenly appreciating and missing such freedoms. This is particularly true among intellectuals, writers, students and, of course, politicians in the opposition. They are seriously writing and debating about various aspects of democracy, and such opinion journals as *Sedae, Shindonga,* and *Sasangge*

Monthly have recently carried many lengthy articles under such titles as " 'Koreanic' Establishment of Democracy," "Democracy and Leadership," and "Democratic Society and Popular Sovereignty." They lament the fact that the Korean people have lost many precious gifts of freedom, partly because they were gifts and not what the nation had won. They are groping for ways of regaining some freedoms that might be compatible with socio-political realities of Korea today and with genuine aspirations of the majority of the people.

It is indeed imprudent to predict the future of democracy in the Third Republic or beyond it. In terms of developmental stages, the disharmonious and exasperating political pattern that had operated within a hurriedly transplanted framework of Western democracy, was abruptly terminated by the military coup. The development since then may be characterized as a stringent and far-reaching reappraisal of indigenous realities and exogenous influences and as a grimly determined launching and operation of a polity that was hoped by the post-coup elites to be congruous with the existing political culture. The first stage lasted for thirteen years, and no one can predict the length of this second stage. It is possible that a synthesis stage will find certain values and practices of Western democracy preserved and upheld in Korea—in the form best suited for the Korean environment.

NOTES, BIBLIOGRAPHY,
AND INDEX

Notes

Chapter 1. Launching the Republic

1. U.S., Congress, Senate, Committee on Foreign Relations, *The United States and the Korean Problem: Documents 1943–1953*, 83rd Cong., 1st sess. (Washington, D.C.: Government Printing Office, 1953), p. 1.

2. U.S., Department of State, *The Record on Korean Unification, 1943–1960: Narrative Summary with Principal Documents* (Washington, D.C.: Government Printing Office, 1960), pp. 5–6.

3. Chong-sik Lee, "Politics in North Korea: Pre-Korean War Stage," *North Korea Today*, ed. Robert A. Scalapino (New York: Praeger, 1963), pp. 9–10.

4. Harry S Truman, *Memoirs* (2 vols.; Garden City: Doubleday, 1956), II, 108–109.

5. Leon Gordenker, *The United Nations and the Peaceful Unification of Korea* (The Hague: Martinus Nijhoff, 1959), p. 13.

6. Truman, *Memoirs*, II, 325–326; Walter S. Millis, ed., *The Forrestal Diaries* (New York: Viking, 1951), pp. 321–322.

7. For a fuller account and a discussion of the United States decision to put the problem of Korea before the General Assembly, see Leland M. Goodrich, *Korea: A Study of U.S. Policy in the United Nations* (New York: Council of Foreign Relations, 1956), pp. 9–30.

8. The full text of the resolution is given in Donald G. Tewks-

bury, ed., *Source Materials on Korean Politics and Ideologies* (New York: Institute of Pacific Relations, 1950), pp. 90–92.

9. "The United States could, with some justification, be accused of giving the United Nations a hot potato, of passing to the international organization a responsibility which the latter was far too weak to assume, and which the United States was unwilling to continue to carry" (Goodrich, *Korea,* p. 41).

10. *Tonga Ilbo* (Seoul), Feb. 12, 1948.

11. For discussions of the divergence of views on elections for a "separate government" in South Korea, see "The Politics of South Korea" and "Wanted: Realistic Settlement," *Voice of Korea* (Washington, D.C.), Feb. 17, 1948. The moderate Kimm Kiusic (Kim Kyu-sik), then the chairman of the South Korean Interim Legislative Assembly, told the Temporary Commission that "any Korean who talks about a South Korean unilateral government will go down in history as a 'bad egg' because once that term is used, the Communists in the North under the direction of the Soviet Union will establish what is called a 'People's Republic or the People's Committee.' Then you will have two unilateral governments in this space of something over 85,000 square miles" (U.N. Doc. A/575, Add. 2, p. 80).

12. Jan. 24, 1948.

13. U.N. Doc. A/583, July 22, 1948.

14. A military government spokesman had estimated that a period of about six months would be required for preparation for the first general elections in Korea (Leon Gordenker, "The United Nations, The United States Occupation and the 1948 Election in Korea," *Political Science Quarterly,* LXXIII, no. 3 [Sept., 1948], 437–438).

15. *Tonga Ilbo,* March 13 and 17, 1948.

16. Kang Chin-hwa, ed., *Taehan minguk kŏnguk simnyŏnji* (The Ten-Year History of the Nation-Building of the Republic of Korea) (Seoul: Kŏnguk simnyŏnji kanhenghoe, 1956), p. 195.

17. For information concerning the conference, see U.N. Docs. A/AC/19/80 and A/AC/19/80, Add. 1. Statements by Kim Ku and Kim Kyu-sik on unity, and the Korean unity conference declaration against southern elections, are given in Tewksbury, *Source Materials,* pp. 95–114.

18. Yi Ki-ha, *Hanguk chŏngdang paltalsa* (A History of the Development of Korean Political Parties) (Seoul: Ŭihoe chŏngch'isa, 1961), pp. 194–195.

19. *Tonga Ilbo*, May 18, 1948. The Labor Party was the Communist organization.

20. U.N. Doc. A/AC/19/66, Add. 3 (Vol. II, Annex VII), quoted in U.S., Senate, *The U.S. and the Korean Problem: 1943–1953*, pp. 18, 21. For a slightly different set of statistics see Republic of Korea, National Assembly, *Taehan minguk kukhoe kaekwan* (Survey of the National Assembly of the Republic of Korea) (Seoul: Minŭiwŏn samuch'ŏ, 1959), p. 4.

21. U.S., Department of State, *Korea 1945 to 1948* (Washington, D.C.: Government Printing Office, 1948), p. 95; italics mine.

22. George M. McCune, "The Korean Situation," *Far Eastern Survey*, XVII, no. 17 (Sept. 8, 1948), 199.

23. U.S., Senate, *The U.S. and the Korean Problem: 1943–1953*, p. 23.

24. U.N., Press Release 70, June 30, 1948.

25. U.S., Department of State, Office of Public Affairs, *Problems of Greece, Korea, and Palestine* (Washington, D.C.: Government Printing Office, 1949), p. 20.

26. U.N., General Assembly, Resolution 195 (III), Dec. 12, 1948. Also discussed in Chŏng Il-hyŏng, *U.N. kwa hanguk munjae* (The U.N. and the Korean Problem) (Seoul: Korean Association for the United Nations, 1961), p. 8.

27. Republic of Korea, National Assembly, *Ch'amgo charyo* (Reference Materials) (Seoul: Minŭiwŏn samuch'ŏ, 1959), XVI, 23–25.

28. Richard C. Allen, *Korea's Syngman Rhee* (Rutland, Vt.: Tuttle, 1960), p. 97.

29. Korea, Assembly, *Ch'amgo charyo*, XVI, 23–25.

30. Kim Yong-sang, "Kukhoeŭi tongt'ewa kŭmhuŭi munje" (The Complexion of the National Assembly and the Problems of the Future), *Shinch'ŏnji*, III, no. 4 (June, 1948), 21.

31. For the complete roster of the elected representatives and their committee assignments, permanent as well as *ad hoc*, see Republic of Korea, National Assembly, *Kukhoe simnyŏnji* (The Ten-Year Record of the National Assembly) (Seoul: Minŭiwŏn samuch'ŏ, 1958), pp. 20–84.

32. Werner Levi, "Fate of Democracy in South and Southeast Asia," *Far Eastern Quarterly*, XXVIII (Feb., 1959), 26.

33. Conlon Associates, Ltd., *United States Foreign Policy: Asia* (Washington, D.C.: Government Printing Office, 1957), p. 56.

34. The Korean National Assembly had not officially adopted an English-language version of the Constitution. The English translation quoted here is from that prepared by the Office of Public Information of the Republic of Korea.

35. Paul S. Dull, "South Korean Constitution," *Far Eastern Survey*, XVII, no. 17 (Sept. 8, 1948), 205.

36. Han T'ae-yŏn, "Chei konghwaguk hŏnbŏpŭi kyŏnghyang" (The Tendency of the Constitution of the Second Republic), *Sasangge Monthly*, VIII, no. 6 (June, 1960), 165–173. Kim Nam-jin, "Sahoe kujowa hŏnbŏp chilsŏ" (Social Structure and Constitutional Order), *Sasangge Monthly*, IX, no. 7 (July, 1961), 50.

37. Thirteen matters were itemized in Article 72.

38. The wording here indicated that the President always had one vote and, in case of a tie, a tie-breaking second vote.

39. Dull, "South Korean Constitution," p. 206.

40. The members of the Constitution-Drafting Committee, headed by Yu Chin-o, were in agreement up to June 20, 1948—less than a month before the Constitution was adopted by the Assembly—on the responsible cabinet system of the new government. On June 20, the drafters were called to the mansion of Dr. Rhee, who had been strongly advocating the adoption of a presidential system. In the two days following their visit with Rhee, the drafters hastily eliminated some features of the cabinet system from their draft, and a new draft was submitted to the Assembly on June 23. Subsequently, the National Assembly adopted this peculiar constitutional machinery, despite some persistent voices raised against the move on the ground that the Constitution was sowing the seeds of authoritarianism (Kim Yong-sang, "Hŏnbŏpŭl ssagodonŭn kukhoe p'ungkyŏng" [The National Assembly Scene on the Problem of the Constitution], *Shinch'ŏnji*, III, no. 6 [July, 1948], 25–26).

41. Dull, "South Korean Constitution," p. 207.

42. Tewksbury, *Source Materials*, p. 117.

Chapter 2. The Republic in Operation

1. Han T'ae-yŏn, "Hanguk yadangŭi sahoehak" (Sociology of the Korean Opposition Parties), *Sasangge Monthly*, VIII, no. 2 (Feb., 1960), 28.

2. Lawrence K. Rosinger, *The State of Asia* (New York: Knopf, 1951), p. 148.

3. *Ibid.*, p. 146.

4. Han T'ae-su, *Hanguk chŏngdangsa* (A History of Korean Political Parties) (Seoul: Sin t'aeyangsa, 1961), p. 113.

5. Sawŏl hyŏngmyŏng ch'ŏngsa p'yŏnch'anhoe, *Sawŏl hyŏngmyŏng ch'ŏngsa* (The Annals of the April Revolution) (Seoul: Sŏnggongsa, 1960), pp. 370–372.

6. Among the very first to go were Foreign Minister Chang T'ek-sang, Home Minister Yun To-hae, and Agriculture Minister Cho Bong-am.

7. Richard C. Allen, *Korea's Syngman Rhee* (Rutland, Vt.: Tuttle, 1960), p. 102.

8. Cho Pyŏng-ok, *Naŭi hoegorok* (My Recollections) (Seoul: Mingyosa, 1959), pp. 172–175. Cho, who was to become a presidential candidate later, was the National Police Director in the military government period. He told the U.N. Temporary Commission in February, 1948, that 25 per cent of the men and 53 per cent of the officers had held police positions under the Japanese (U.N. Doc. A/575, Add. 2, p. 117).

9. Sawŏl hyŏngmyŏng ch'ŏngsa p'yŏnch'anhoe, *Sawŏl hyŏngmyŏng ch'ŏngsa*, p. 372.

10. The text of the law is given in *Voice of Korea* (Washington, D.C.), Dec. 15, 1948.

11. Rosinger, *State of Asia*, p. 149.

12. *Tonga Ilbo* (Seoul), Dec. 8, 1948.

13. Rhee's message to the National Assembly on March 31, 1949.

14. *Voice of Korea*, Dec. 15, 1948.

15. *New York Times*, June 28, 1949.

16. *Tonga Ilbo*, July 2, 1949. Kim's assassin, Lieutenant An Tu-hi, was kept incommunicado by the military police, tried in

secret by the military court presided over by Lieutenant General Wŏn Yong-dŏk, and sentenced to life imprisonment. An, however, served only about three years of his term; he was pardoned at some time during the Korean War and was restored to active military duty. He eventually rose to the rank of colonel and finally retired to civilian life.

17. Donald G. Tewksbury, ed., *Source Materials on Korean Politics and Ideologies* (New York: Institute of Pacific Relations, 1950), p. 145.

18. *Ibid.*

19. Conlon Associates, Ltd., *United States Foreign Policy: Asia* (Washington, D.C.: Government Printing Office, 1957), p. 100.

20. Yi Ki-ha, *Hanguk chŏngdang paltalsa* (A History of the Development of Korean Political Parties) (Seoul: Ŭihoe chŏngch'isa, 1961), pp. 204–205.

21. Han T'ae-su, "Hanguk yadangŭi sahoehak," p. 117. For a text of the proposed amendments, see *Tonga Ilbo*, Jan. 28, 1950.

22. *Voice of Korea*, May 27, 1950.

23. Yi Ki-ha, *Hanguk chŏngdang paltalsa*, p. 213.

24. *Constitutional Dictatorship: Crisis Government in Modern Democracies* (Princeton: Princeton University Press, 1948), p. 6.

25. U.S., Agency for International Development, *U.S. Foreign Assistance and Assistance from International Organizations* (Washington, D.C.: Government Printing Office, 1962), p. 64.

26. Ch'oe Ŭng-sang, *Nongjŏng simnyŏnsa* (The Ten-Year History of the Administration of Agriculture) (Seoul: Semunsa, 1959), pp. 126–38.

27. The most notorious of these bloodbaths was the "Kŏch'ang Incident" in which about six hundred men and women, young and old, were herded into a narrow valley and mowed down with machine guns by a South Korean army unit in February, 1951—at the height of the Korean War.

28. U.S., Department of State, *A Historical Summary of United States–Korean Relations: With a Chronology of Important Developments 1834–1962* (Washington, D.C.: Government Printing Office, 1962), p. 74.

29. U.S., Congress, Senate, Committee on Foreign Relations, *The United States and the Korean Problem: Documents 1943–1953*, pp. 26–27.

30. *Ibid.*, pp. 29, 32.

31. U.S., Agency for International Development, *Foreign Assistance*, p. 64.

32. Harry S. Truman, *Memoirs* (2 vols.; Garden City: Doubleday, 1956), II, 336; italics mine. While Rhee called Korea a "bulwark of democracy in the east," Walter Lippmann characterized the South Korean government as one "dominated by reactionaries" (*New York Herald Tribune*, July 27, 1950).

33. Truman, *Memoirs*, II, 337.

34. *Ibid.*

35. *New York Times*, June 27, 1950.

36. Sin Sŏk-ho, "Chayudang sŏngnip ijŏnŭi chŏngjŏng" (The Political Situation before the Formation of the Liberal Party), in Hanguk hyŏngmyŏng chaep'ansa p'yŏnch'an wiwŏnhoe, *Hanguk hyŏngmyŏng chaep'ansa* (The History of Revolutionary Trials in Korea) (Seoul: Hanguk hyŏngmyŏng chaep'ansa p'yŏnch'an wiwŏnhoe, 1962), I, 12.

37. Conlon Associates, *U.S. Foreign Policy: Asia*, p. 11; Stephen Bradner, "Korea: Experiment and Instability," *Japan Quarterly*, VIII, no. 4 (Oct.–Dec., 1961), 419.

38. Allen, *Korea's Syngman Rhee*, p. 138; Han T'ae-yŏn, "Hanguk yadangŭi sahoehak," p. 127; Yi Ki-ha, *Hanguk chŏngdang paltalsa*, pp. 218–219.

39. Hakwŏnsa, *Korea: Its Land, People and Culture of All Ages* (Seoul: Hakwŏnsa, 1960), p. 132.

40. Cho Il-mun, "Chŏngch'i p'adongŭi insikkwa pip'an" (An Understanding and Criticism of the Political Crisis), *Shinch'ŏnji*, III, no. 1 (April, 1953), 32.

41. *Ibid.*, p. 33.

42. "Instead of the free expression of genuine popular will, creations of popular will took place too often in Korea" (Yi Kŭkch'an, "Chŏngch'ijŏk mugwansimkwa minjujuŭi wigi" [Political Apathy and the Crisis of Democracy], *Sasangge Monthly*, IX, no. 4 [April, 1961], 68).

43. For a more detailed presentation of the political situation in Pusan in this period, see Kang Chin-hwa, ed., *Taehan minguk kŏnguk simnyŏnji* (The Ten-Year History of the Nation-Building of the Republic of Korea) (Seoul: Kŏnguk simnyŏnji kanhenghoe, 1956), pp. 221–223.

44. *New York Times*, May 28, 1952.

45. Allen, *Korea's Syngman Rhee*, p. 144.

46. Cho Pyŏng-ok (Chough Pyong-ok), *Minjujuŭiwa na* (Democracy and I) (Seoul: Yŏngsin munhwasa, 1959), p. 167.

47. Allen, *Korea's Syngman Rhee*, p. 149.

48. Republic of Korea, National Assembly, *Taehan minguk kukhoe kaekwan* (Survey of the National Assembly of the Republic of Korea) (Seoul: Minŭiwŏn samuch'o, 1959), p. 7.

49. Kang Chin-hwa, *Taehan minguk kŏnguk simnyŏnji*, p. 244.

50. Rhee with 5,238,769 votes, about 72 per cent of the popular vote, and Ham with 2,934,813 votes. Two other presidential candidates obtained tiny fractions of the number attained by Rhee: Cho Bong-am, the former Minister of Agriculture, received 797,594 votes, and Yi Si-yŏng, the former Vice-President, 764,725 votes. Among the unsuccessful vice-presidential candidates, Cho Pyŏng-ok received 575,260 votes, and Chŏn Chin-han 302,471 votes.

51. David M. Earl, "Korea: The Meaning of the Second Republic," *Far Eastern Survey*, XXIX, no. 11 (Nov., 1960), 170.

52. Chu Sŏk-kyun, "T'am-o ron" (Essay on Corrupt Officials), *Sasangge Monthly*, I, no. 5 (Aug., 1953), 178.

53. Sin Sŏk-ho, "Chayudang sŏngnip ijonŭi chŏngjŏng," p. 14.

54. *Ibid.*, p. 71.

55. Allen, *Korea's Syngman Rhee*, p. 205.

56. Sin Sŏk-ho, "Chayudang sŏngnip ijonŭi chŏngjŏng," p. 74.

57. Cho Pyŏng-ok, *Naŭi hoegorok*, p. 358.

58. Allen, *Korea's Syngman Rhee*, pp. 204–205.

59. Ŏm Sang-sŏp, *Kwŏllyŏkkwa chayu* (Authority and Freedom) (Seoul: Kyŏngku ch'ulpansa, 1957), pp. 41–42.

60. Korea, Assembly, *Taehan minguk kukhoe kaekwan*, p. 8.

Chapter 3. Autocracy and the Student Uprising

1. For a detailed study of political parties in South Korea from 1945 to 1966, see Yi Ki-ha, *Hanguk chŏngdang paltalsa* (A History of the Development of Korean Political Parties) (Seoul: Ŭihoe chŏngch'isa, 1961), pp. 37–252.

2. Cho Pyŏng-ok, *Naŭi hoegorok* (My Recollections) (Seoul: Mingyosa, 1959), p. 377.

3. Cho Bong-am was subsequently executed on July 31, 1959, in Seoul. Cho was arrested with twenty of his supporters shortly before the May, 1956, elections. In the following July he was sentenced to five years' imprisonment for illegal possession of arms and a minor violation of security regulations. At a second trial, in February, 1959, he was charged with advocating peaceful unification of Korea (by implication, on Communist terms); the charge was later varied to complicity with North Korea and he was sentenced to death. Appeals after both trials were rejected. The prosecution and the government spokesman made much of the fact that Cho had once been a Communist. He was said to have left the party in 1946, however, and Rhee himself had appointed him Minister of Agriculture in his first cabinet in 1948. The Seoul newspapers of August 1, 1959, gave prominent space to the execution, but at noon the national police chief, Yi Kang-hak, announced that any further reports would constitute a violation of security regulations.

4. Richard C. Allen, *Korea's Syngman Rhee* (Rutland, Vt.: Tuttle, 1960), p. 214.

5. Kim Yong-sŏn, "Kukhoe sŏngŏ" (National Assembly Elections), *Sasangge Monthly*, IV, no. 8 (Aug., 1956), 62.

6. David M. Earl, "Korea: The Meaning of the Second Republic," *Far Eastern Survey*, XXIX, no. 11 (Nov., 1960), 171. On September 19, 1956, a would-be assassin wounded Chang slightly as he was leaving a Democratic Party rally in Seoul, thus prompting him to go into virtual seclusion for the next two years or so. For a detailed account of the plots by Liberal Party members leading up to the assassination attempt, see Sawŏl hyŏngmyŏng ch'ŏngsa p'yŏnch'anhoe, *Sawŏl hyŏngmyŏng ch'ŏngsa* (The Annals of the April Revolution) (Seoul: Sŏnggongsa, 1960), pp. 444–448.

7. Han T'ae-yŏn, "Hanguk yadangŭi sahoehak" (Sociology of the Korean Opposition Parties), *Sasangge Monthly*, VIII, no. 2 (Feb., 1960), 25.

8. Yun Ch'ŏn-ju, "Pujŏng sŏngŏŭi pangjŏngsik" (Formulae for Rigged Elections), *Sasangge Monthly*, VIII, no. 7 (June, 1960), 112.

9. *Ibid.*

10. Allen, *Korea's Syngman Rhee*, p. 223.

11. Sin Sŏk-ho, "Chayudang sŏngnip ijŏnŭi chŏngjŏng" (The Political Situation before the Formation of the Liberal Party), in Hanguk hyŏngmyŏng chaep'ansa p'yŏnch'an wiwŏnhoe, *Hanguk hyŏngmyŏng chaep'ansa* (The History of Revolutionary Trials in Korea) (Seoul: Hanguk hyŏngmyŏng chaep'ansa p'yŏnch'an wiwŏnhoe, 1962), I, 97.

12. *Ibid.*, p. 99.

13. Allen, *Korea's Syngman Rhee*, p. 223.

14. Article 1 of the National Security Law, Republic of Korea, Law No. 500. The excerpts from the law cited here are from an unofficial translation of the law by the Far Eastern Division of the Library of Congress, Washington, D.C. The Korean original was printed in *Kwanpo* (Official Gazette), no. 2206, Dec. 26, 1958.

15. Cho Pyŏng-ok, *Minjujuŭiwa na* (Democracy and I) (Seoul: Yŏngsin munhwasa, 1959), p. 267.

16. For statements of the opposition leaders, Cho Pyŏng-ok and Chang Myŏn, on the question, see *Kyŏnghyang Shinmun* (Seoul), Dec. 26, 1958.

17. Allen, *Korea's Syngman Rhee*, p. 224.

18. For excerpts from a 71-page letter from the Democratic Party to the Central Election Committee exposing alleged irregular election plans of the Liberal Party, see *Voice of Korea* (Washington, D.C.), April, 1960, and Allen, *Korea's Syngman Rhee*, p. 226.

19. Republic of Korea, Ministry of Foreign Affairs, *The Military Revolution in Korea* (Seoul: Taehan minguk oemubu, 1961), p. 6. Much of this maneuvering was also quite apparent to foreign observers. For instance, see John M. Barr, "The Second Republic of Korea," *Far Eastern Survey*, XXIX, no. 9 (Sept., 1960), 130.

20. Sin Sŏk-ho, "Chayudang sŏngnip ijŏnŭi chŏngjŏng," p. 106.

21. Barr, "Second Republic," p. 130.

22. Kang In-sŏp, "Sawŏl hyŏngmyŏng hugi" (A Postscript to the April Revolution), *Shindonga*, April, 1965, pp. 80–81.

23. Cho T'ak-sŏng, ed., *Sawŏl hyŏngmyŏng* (April Revolution) (Seoul: Ch'angwŏnsa, 1960), p. 60; Min Yong-bin, ed.,

Sawŏlŭi yŏngungdŭl (April Heroes) (Seoul: Ilsinsa, 1960), p. 46.

24. Korean Research and Information Office, *Korea Report: Reports from the Cabinet Ministers of the Republic of Korea*, VI (Washington, D.C.: Korean Research and Information Office, 1959), 104–106.

25. Kang In-sŏp, "Sawŏl hyŏngmyŏng hugi," pp. 81–82.

26. Sin Sŏk-ho, "Chayudang sŏngnip ijŏnŭi chŏngjŏng," p. 140.

27. The order to fire was given by the then Home Minister, Hong Jin-gi (Hanguk hyŏngmyŏng chaep'ansa p'yŏnch'an wiwŏnhoe, *Hanguk hyŏngmyŏng chaep'ansa*, II, 1054–1069).

28. By the time the Rhee regime was toppled, the uprising had claimed 183 lives, wounding 6,259 (Yi Ki-ha, *Hanguk chŏngdang paltalsa*, p. 437).

29. U.S., Department of State, Historical Office, *American Foreign Policy: Current Documents 1960* (Washington, D.C.: Government Printing Office, 1964), p. 680.

30. *Ibid.*

31. Sin Sŏk-ho, "Chayudang sŏngnip ijŏnŭi chŏngjŏng," p. 143.

32. Yi Ki-ha, *Hanguk chŏngdang paltalsa*, pp. 439–440.

33. Sin Sang-ch'o, "Yi Sŭng-man p'okchŏngŭi chongyŏn" (The End of the Tyranny of Syngman Rhee), *Sasangge Monthly*, VIII, no. 6 (June, 1960), 84.

34. Kang In-sŏp, "Sawŏl hyŏngmyŏng hugi," pp. 89–90.

35. Cho Ka-gyŏng, "Hyŏngmyŏng chuch'aeŭi chŏngsinjŏk honmi" (Spiritual Confusion of the Main Body of the Revolution), *Sasangge Monthly*, IX, no. 4 (April, 1961), 70–79.

36. Personal interviews with the former Defense Minister Kim Chong-yŏl and General Song Yo-ch'an.

37. Released on September 15, 1960; quoted in Earl, "Korea," p. 173.

38. Min Sŏk-hong, "Hyŏndaesawa chayu minjujuŭi: Sawŏl hyŏngmyŏngŭi ihaelŭl wihayŏ" (Contemporary History and Liberal Democracy: For an Understanding of the April Revolution), *Sasangge Monthly*, VIII, no. 6 (June, 1960), 96.

39. Hong Sung-chick, "A Pilot Study of the Korean Students' Values," *Korean Affairs*, II, no. 1 (1963), 1–11.

40. Cho Ka-gyŏng, "Hyŏngmyŏng chuch'aeŭi chŏngsinjŏk honmi," p. 71.

41. Hong Isŏp, "Sawŏl hyŏngmyŏngŭi chaep'yŏngka" (Reappraisal of the April Revolution), *Sasangge Monthly*, IX, no. 4 (April, 1961), 55.

42. Kim Sŏng-t'ae, "Sawŏl sipkuilŭi simnihak" (Psychology of April 19), *Sasangge Monthly*, IX, no. 4 (April, 1961), 80–81. The total number of students interviewed is not given in the article. It should be noted that each student gave more than one of the reasons named by the professor.

43. C. I. Eugene Kim and Kim Ke-soo, "The April 1960 Student Movement," *A Pattern of Political Development: Korea*, ed. C. I. Eugene Kim (Kalamazoo, Mich.: Korea Research and Publications, 1964), p. 55.

Chapter 4. Democracy in the Second Republic

1. In less than a year after the third series of amendments, the Constitution was "suspended" in the wake of the military coup of May 16, 1961.

2. Han T'ae-yŏn, "Chei konghwaguk hŏnbŏpŭi kyŏnghyang" (The Tendency of the Constitution of the Second Republic), *Sasangge Monthly*, VIII, no. 6 (June, 1960), 165–173.

3. Quotations from the Constitution of the Second Republic are from a "tentative translation" of the document by the Republic of Korea, Ministry of Foreign Affairs, published in August, 1960.

4. John M. Barr, "The Second Republic of Korea," *Far Eastern Survey*, XXIX, no. 9 (Sept., 1960), 131.

5. Sŏ Pyŏng-jo, *Chukwŏnjaŭi chŭngŏn: Hanguk taeŭi chŏngch'isa* (Testimonies of the Sovereign: A History of Representative Government in Korea) (Seoul: Moŭm ch'ulpansa, 1963), p. 352.

6. *Voice of Korea* (Washington, D.C.), June–July, 1960.

7. For the names of those who broke with the Liberal Party on June 1 and the quick disintegration of the Liberal Party, see *Kyŏnghyang Shinmun* (Seoul), June 2, 1960.

8. *Ibid.*, June 10 and 23, 1960; Sŏ Pyŏng-jo, *Chukwŏnjaŭi chŭngŏn*, p. 362.

9. *Kyŏnghyang Shinmun*, June 24, 1960.

10. The New Faction occupied 92 seats, and the rest went to the Old Faction, as of July 31, 1960.

11. Sŏ Pyŏng-jo, *Chukwŏnjaŭi chŭngŏn*, p. 367.

12. *Ibid.*, pp. 365–366.

13. *Voice of Korea*, Sept.–Oct., 1960.

14. According to Ambassador McConaughy's replies on August 3 to a written questionnaire submitted by the Associated Press.

15. Sŏ Pyŏng-jo, *Chukwŏnjaŭi chŭngŏn*, p. 377.

16. David M. Earl, "Korea: The Meaning of the Second Republic," *Far Eastern Survey*, XXIX, no. 11 (Nov., 1960), 174.

17. *Ibid.*, p. 175.

18. *Tonga Ilbo* (Seoul), Nov. 8–9, 1960.

19. Sin Sŏk-ho, "Chayudang sŏngnip ijŏnŭi chŏngjŏng" (The Political Situation before the Formation of the Liberal Party), in Hanguk hyŏngmyŏng chaep'ansa p'yŏnch'an wiwŏnhoe, *Hanguk hyŏngmyŏng chaep'ansa* (The History of Revolutionary Trials in Korea) (Seoul: Hanguk hyŏngmyŏng chaep'ansa p'yŏnch'an wiwŏnhoe, 1962), I, 197; Sŏ Pyŏng-jo, *Chukwŏnjaŭi chŭngŏn*, p. 435.

20. Hahn Bae-ho and Kim Kyu-taik, "Korean Political Leaders (1952–1962): Their Social Origins and Skills," *Asian Survey*, III, no. 7 (July, 1963), 320.

21. C. N. Weems, "Korea: Dilemma of an Underdeveloped Country," *Foreign Policy Association Headline Series*, no. 144 (Nov.–Dec., 1960), p. 39.

22. *Tonga Ilbo*, Dec. 28, 1960.

23. *Ibid.*

24. Sŏ Pyŏng-jo, *Chukwŏnjaŭi chŭngŏn*, p. 429.

25. W. D. Reeve, *The Republic of Korea: A Political and Economic Study* (London: Oxford University Press, 1963), p. 139.

26. Richard C. Allen, "South Korea: The New Regime," *Pacific Affairs*, XXXIV, no. 1 (Spring, 1961), 54.

27. Stephen Bradner, "Korea: Experiment and Instability," *Japan Quarterly*, VIII, no. 4 (Oct.–Dec., 1961), 414.

28. The text is from the translation by the Korean Ministry of Foreign Affairs.

29. *Kyŏnghyang Shinmun*, Oct. 12, 1960.

30. Republic of Korea, Law No. 587, in Ch'ŏngyang yukbŏp p'yŏnch'an wiwŏnhoe, *Yukbŏp chŏnsŏ* (Complete Six Codes) (Seoul: Chŏngyang Codification Committee of the Six Codes, 1961), pp. 28–30. No official translation of this law is available at present.

31. The so-called "automatic cases" numbered 690, according to an announcement by the Ministry of Justice on February 25, 1961. For their names, see *Kyŏnghyang Shinmun*, Feb. 25, 1961.

32. *Kyŏnghyang Shinmun*, Dec. 31, 1960.

33. Allen, "South Korea," p. 55.

34. Bradner, "Korea," p. 414.

35. *Ibid.*

36. Sin Sŏk-ho, "Chayudang sŏngnip ijŏnŭi chŏngjŏng," p. 258.

37. *Kyŏnghyang Shinmun*, Jan. 31, 1961.

38. *Tonga Ilbo*, Dec. 8, 1960.

39. Hong Isŏp, "Sawŏl hyŏngmyŏngŭi chaep'yŏngka" (Re-appraisal of the April Revolution), *Sasangge Monthly*, IX, no. 4 (April, 1961), 12–13. For Premier Chang's own appraisal of political developments in the Second Republic, see his brief written statement, "On the State of My Mind," issued on August 16, 1961 (*Tonga Ilbo*, Aug. 16, 1961). The statement was written about three months after the May, 1961, *coup d'état* overthrew his regime and while he was reported to be under house arrest.

40. *Tonga Ilbo*, Dec. 2, 1960.

41. Yi Kŭk-ch'an, "Chŏng'ch'ijok mugwansimkwa minjujuŭi wigi" (Political Apathy and the Crisis of Democracy), *Sasangge Monthly*, IX, no. 4 (April, 1961), 62.

42. Harold W. Sunoo, "Possibility of 'Koreanic' Democracy," *Korea Journal*, I, no. 1 (Sept., 1961), 5.

43. Home Minister Shin Hyŏn-don stated on February 23, 1961, that leftist elements, with the backing of Communist Koreans residing in Japan who were financed by the North Korean regime, were planning an antigovernment uprising either in March or in April. On February 25, however, Premier Chang announced in the House of Representatives that there was no concrete evidence to substantiate the rumors of imminent crisis (*Kyŏnghyang Shinmun*, Feb. 23, 25, 1961).

Chapter 5. The 1961 *Coup d'Etat*

1. John Kie-chiang Oh, "Post-coup Korea on a Treadmill: A Political Analysis," *East-West Center Review,* II, no. 2 (Oct., 1965), 2–3.

2. The retirement of General Chŏng Il-kwŏn from active military service at the age of forty and his appointment as Ambassador to Turkey in May, 1957, may be cited as an example.

3. Hanguk kunsa hyŏngmyŏngsa p'yŏnch'an wiwŏnhoe, *Hanguk kunsa hyŏngmyŏngsa* (The History of the Korean Military Revolution) (Seoul: Tonga sŏjŏk hoesa, 1963), I, 195.

4. Hanguk hyŏngmyŏng chaep'ansa p'yŏnch'an wiwŏnhoe, *Hanguk hyŏngmyŏng chaep'ansa* (The History of Revolutionary Trials in Korea) (Seoul: Hanguk hyŏngmyŏng chaep'ansa p'yŏnch'an wiwŏnhoe, 1962), I, 914–915.

5. Kang In-sŏp, "Yuksa p'algi seng" (The Eighth Graduating Class of the Military Academy), *Shindonga,* Sept., 1964, pp. 170–198.

6. "Military Purification Movement Leads to 1961 May Revolution," *Korean Report,* II, no. 4 (May, 1962), 10. Hereinafter referred to as the "Military Purification Movement."

7. These eleven officers were: O Ch'i-sŏng, Kim Hyŏng-uk, Kil Chae-ho, Yi T'aek-kyun, Ok Ch'ang-ho, Sŏk Chŏng-sŏn, Kim Chong-p'il, Kim Tong-hwan, Kim Tal-hun, Sŏk Ch'ang-hi, and Shin Yun-ch'ang.

8. Hanguk hyŏngmyŏng chaep'ansa p'yŏnch'an wiwŏnhoe, *Hanguk hyŏngmyŏng chaep'ansa,* I, 917.

9. Hanguk kunsa hyŏngmyŏngsa p'yŏnch'an wiwŏnhoe, *Hanguk kunsa hyŏngmyŏngsa,* I, 197–204.

10. Republic of Korea, Supreme Council for National Reconstruction, *Military Revolution in Korea* (Seoul: The Secretariat, Supreme Council for National Reconstruction, 1961), p. 17.

11. Kunsa hyŏngmyŏngsa p'yŏnch'an wiwŏnhoe, *Oilyuk kunsa hyŏngmyŏngŭi chŏnmo* (The Entire Picture of the Military Revolution of May 16) (Seoul: Munkwansa, 1964), p. 294.

12. Hanguk kunsa hyŏngmyŏngsa p'yŏnch'an wiwŏnhoe, *Hanguk kunsa hyŏngmyŏngsa,* IV, 387–400.

13. Kang In-sŏp, "Minjudang chŏngkwŏn ch'oehuŭi nal" (The Last Day of the Democratic Regime), *Shindonga*, May, 1965, pp. 100–101.

14. *Ibid.*

15. Hanguk kunsa hyŏngmyŏngsa p'yŏnch'an wiwŏnhoe, *Hanguk kunsa hyŏngmyŏngsa*, I-B, 4–5.

16. *Korean Times* (Seoul), May 17, 1961.

17. Korea, Supreme Council for National Reconstruction, *Military Revolution*, p. i.

18. Walter Briggs, "The Military Revolution in Korea: On Its Leader and Achievements," *Koreana Quarterly*, V, no. 2 (Summer, 1963), 28.

19. Hanguk kunsa hyŏngmyŏngsa p'yŏnch'an wiwŏnhoe, *Hanguk kunsa hyŏngmyŏngsa*, I-A, 260.

20. Briggs, "Military Revolution," p. 29.

21. *Ibid.*, pp. 22–23.

22. *Ibid.*, p. 31.

23. Hanguk kunsa hyŏngmyŏngsa p'yŏnch'an wiwŏnhoe, *Hanguk kunsa hyŏngmyŏngsa*, I-A, 252.

24. Yi Han-lim was a graduate of the Military Academy of Manchukuo under the Japanese domination, as was General Chung Hee Park. General Yi also attended the U.S. Army Infantry School at Fort Benning, Georgia.

25. *Korean Times*, May 18, 1961.

26. Personal interviews in Washington, D.C., June, 1961.

27. United Press International, Washington, D.C., May 17, 1961.

28. U.S., Department of State, Historical Office, *American Foreign Policy: Current Documents 1961* (Washington, D.C.: Government Printing Office, 1965), p. 974. Italics mine.

29. United Press International, Washington, D.C., May 19, 1961.

30. *Ibid.* Italics mine.

31. U.S., State Department, *American Foreign Policy: Current Documents 1961*, p. 975.

32. *Ibid.*

Chapter 6. Rule by the Military Junta

1. Republic of Korea, Supreme Council for National Reconstruction, *Military Revolution in Korea* (Seoul: The Secretariat, Supreme Council for National Reconstruction, 1961), pp. 149–156. The Supreme Council for National Reconstruction Law, promulgated on June 10, defined the organizational features of the Council as an institution (*ibid.*, pp. 157–169).

2. The total budget for 1961 was 624.3 billion hwan.

3. For a complete list of the supreme councilors, see Hanguk kunsa hyŏngmyŏngsa p'yŏnch'an wiwŏnhoe, *Hanguk kunsa hyŏngmyŏngsa* (The History of the Korean Military Revolution) (Seoul: Tonga sŏjŏk hoesa, 1963), I-B, 4.

4. *Ibid.*, p. 4.

5. *Ibid.*, pp. 11–13.

6. *Ibid.*, p. 12.

7. W. D. Reeve, *The Republic of Korea: A Political and Economic Study* (London: Oxford University Press, 1963), p. 150.

8. Republic of Korea, Ministry of Foreign Affairs, *The Military Revolution in Korea* (Seoul: Taehan minguk ŏemubu, 1961), p. 12.

9. *Ibid.*, pp. 12–13.

10. Hanguk kunsa hyŏngmyŏngsa p'yŏnch'an wiwŏnhoe, *Hanguk kunsa hyŏngmyŏngsa*, I-B, 610.

11. *Republic of Korea*, p. 153.

12. It was at about 4:30 P.M., May 16, that Chang finally accepted the chairmanship (Walter Briggs, "The Military Revolution in Korea: On Its Leader and Achievements," *Koreana Quarterly*, V, no. 2 [Summer, 1963], 33).

13. General Chang and his secretary were sentenced to death on January 10, 1962, by the Revolutionary Court, and twenty-two of his fellow officers were given terms of imprisonment. Subsequently, the appeals board reduced these sentences; although General Chang was found guilty of counterrevolutionary activities, he was sentenced to life imprisonment, while three of his fellow officers were acquitted. However, on May 2, 1962, General Park ordered the release of General Chang and seven others in

view of their contribution to the success of the military revolution in its initial state (Reeve, *Republic of Korea*, p. 154; Hanguk hyŏngmyŏng chaep'ansa p'yŏnch'an wiwŏnhoe, *Hanguk hyŏngmyŏng chaep'ansa* [The History of Revolutionary Trials in Korea] [Seoul: Hanguk hyŏngmyŏng chaep'ansa p'yŏnch'an wiwŏnhoe, 1962], I, 1013–1014, IV, 435–688).

14. Personal interviews, Washington, D.C., May, 1961.

15. "Biographical Sketch of General Chung Hee Park," *Korean Observer*, Aug., 1963, p. 5.

16. Paek Nam-ju, ed., *Hyŏngmyŏng chidoja Pak Chŏng-hi non* (On Chung Hee Park, the Revolutionary Leader) (Seoul: Inmulkaesa, 1961), pp. 39–42.

17. Paek Nam-ju, *Hyŏngmyŏng chidoja Pak Chŏng-hi non*, p. 60.

18. *Ibid.*, pp. 61–62.

19. *Supra*, Chapter 2.

20. Paek Nam-ju, *Hyŏngmyŏng chidoja Pak Chŏng-hi non*, pp. 56–57.

21. Chŏng Chae-ho, "Pak Chŏng-hi," *Saedae*, III, no. 3 (April, 1965), 138.

22. *Chidojado* (Seoul: Kukka chaekŏn ch'oego hoeŭi, 1961); *Uri minjokŭi nagalkil* (Seoul: Tonga ch'ulp'ansa, 1962); *Kukkawa hyŏngmyŏngkwa na* (Seoul: Hyangmunsa, 1963), trans. Leon Sinder as *The Country, the Revolution and I*.

23. *Chidojado*, pp. 18–33.

24. *Ibid.*, pp. 23–25.

25. *Ibid.*, p. 24.

26. *Ibid.*, p. 26.

27. *Korean Affairs*, II (May–June, 1962), 111–121.

28. *Ibid.*, p. 112. Again, this is a direct quotation from a translation.

29. *Ibid.*, p. 113.

30. *The Country, the Revolution and I*, pp. 107–108.

31. "Korean Political Philosophy," p. 117.

32. *Ibid.*, pp. 119–120.

33. *Ibid.*, p. 121.

34. *The Country, the Revolution and I*, p. 105.

35. *Ibid.*

36. *Ibid.*, p. 57.

37. *Ibid.*, pp. 105–108.
38. *Ibid.*, p. 59.
39. Hanguk kunsa hyŏngmyŏngsa p'yŏnch'an wiwŏnhoe, *Hanguk kunsa hyŏngmyŏngsa*, I-B, 652–653.
40. In addition to Lieutenant General Yi Chu-il, head of the committee, the members were Major General Yu Yang-su, Marine Major General Kim Tong-ha, Brigadier General Cho Chi-hyŏng, Brigadier General Son Ch'ang-kyu, Marine Brigadier General Kim Yun-gŭn, and Colonel Yi Sŏk-jae.
41. *Korea Informer* (Seoul), July–Aug., 1962, p. 17.
42. *The Country, the Revolution and I*, p. 60.
43. Robert A. Scalapino, "Korea: The Politics of Change," *Asian Survey*, III, no. 1 (Jan., 1963), p. 36.
44. Reeve, *Republic of Korea*, p. 165.
45. *Ibid.*, p. 168.
46. *The Country, the Revolution and I*, pp. 146–148.
47. Haptong News Agency, *Korea Annual 1964* (Seoul: Haptong News Agency, 1964), p. 291.
48. *Ibid.*, p. 137.

Chapter 7. The Politics of Restoration

1. Statement read by General Park at a news conference in Seoul, Aug. 2, 1961.
2. U.N. Doc. A/4900, p. 7, and U.S., Department of State, Historical Office, *American Foreign Policy: Current Documents 1961* (Washington, D.C.: Government Printing Office, 1965), p. 977.
3. Kim Yŏng-su, " 'Minju konghwadang' sajŏn chojik" (The Advance Organization of the "Democratic Republican Party"), *Shindonga*, Nov., 1964, pp. 168–173.
4. *Ibid.*, pp. 173–176.
5. *Ibid.*, p. 187.
6. Kim Ki-bŏm, "Certain Features of the Constitution," *Korean Affairs*, III, no. 1 (April, 1964), 20; Han Tai-soo, "Results of National Referendum and Its Significance," *Koreana Quarterly*, V, no. 1 (April, 1963), 7.
7. Kim Ki-bŏm, "Certain Features," pp. 21–22.

8. *Korean Republic Weekly*, Jan. 2, 1963.

9. *Ibid.*

10. *Ibid.*

11. Yu Hyŏk-in, "Pak taet'ongnyŏngŭl umjiginŭn saramdŭl" (Those Who Move President Park), *Shindonga*, Oct., 1964, pp. 158–159.

12. Hanguk kunsa hyŏngmyŏngsa p'yŏnch'an wiwŏnhoe, *Hanguk hunsa hyŏngmyŏngsa* (The History of the Korean Military Revolution) (Seoul: Tonga sŏjŏk hoesa, 1963), I-B, 662–664.

13. Yu Hyŏk-in, "Pak taet'ongnyŏngŭl umjiginŭn saramdŭl," pp. 158–159.

14. United Press International, Washington, D.C., Feb. 18, 1963.

15. *Korea Times* (Seoul), March 17, 1963.

16. *Ibid.*, March 27, 1963.

17. United Press International, Washington, D.C., March 25, 1963.

18. These quotations from the constitutional text are from an undated English translation by the Office of Legislation, Republic of Korea.

19. Kim Ki-bŏm, "Certain Features," p. 23.

20. Republic of Korea, Supreme Council for National Reconstruction, *A Commentary on the Constitution of the Republic of Korea As Submitted to National Referendum* (Seoul: n. pub., 1962), p. 12.

21. Kim Myong-whai, "The Presidential Election in Korea, 1963," *Korean Affairs*, II, nos. 3–4 (Oct., 1963), 372.

22. Korea, Supreme Council for National Reconstruction, *Commentary*, pp. 33–34.

23. Yim Hong-bin, "An Analysis of the General Election in 1963," *Korean Affairs*, III, no. 1 (April, 1964), 124.

24. *Ibid.*, p. 125.

25. U.N., General Assembly, *Official Records*, 18th sess., supp. no. 12A–A5512, Add. 1.

26. Yim Hong-bin, "An Analysis," p. 121.

27. *Ibid.*, pp. 122–123.

28. *Ibid.*, p. 125.

29. Hanguk kunsa hyŏngmyŏngsa p'yŏnch'an wiwŏnhoe, *Hanguk kunsa hyŏngmyŏngsa*, I-B, 655–680.

30. Lee Joung-sik, "The Social Origin of Members of the

Sixth National Assembly," *Korean Affairs*, III, no. 1 (April, 1964), 15.

Postscript

1. Yi Chŏng-sik, "Cheyukde taet'ongnyŏng sŏnkŏŭi ŭii" (The Significance of the Sixth Presidential Elections), *Shindonga*, June, 1967, pp. 69–72. Professor Yi, of the Tonguk University in Seoul, believes that this emphasis is a departure from the pattern under the Democratic regime of Premier Chang, which posited the twin goals of the development of a democratic political system and a rapid economic development within such a political framework.

2. Regarding Yun's individual visits with Yu Chin-o, Paek Nak-jun, and Yi Pŏm-sŏk and subsequent "meetings of the four," see *Tonga Ilbo* (Seoul), Jan. 26, 28, 30, and 31, 1967.

3. *New York Times*, Feb. 13, 1967.

4. Kim Tae-jung, spokesman of the New Democratic Party, charged that the government and the ruling party were engaged in a shameless "intelligence politics," encouraging activities of splinter parties in order to divide and conquer the opposition. He declared that he "knew that presidential candidates of certain splinter parties twice received sizable amounts of funds" from sources he did not specify. This charge was vehemently denied by Sin Tong-jun, spokesman of the ruling party (*Tonga Ilbo* [Seoul], March 18, 1967).

5. *Japan Times*, April 4, 1967.

6. *Tonga Ilbo*, March 28, 1967.

7. *Ibid.*, May 20, 1967. The exchange ratio between the United States dollar and the Korean won was about 1 to 260 at this time.

8. The commission consists of members from Turkey, Australia, Thailand, the Philippines, Chile, Pakistan, and the Netherlands.

9. May 9, 1967.

10. May 4 and 7, 1967.

11. Chung Young-iob, "Economic Development and Population Growth in South Korea during 1953–1971" (unpublished paper presented to the 16th annual meeting of the Midwest Conference on Asian Affairs, Nov., 1967), p. 3.

12. Bank of Korea, *Economic Statistical Yearbook 1966* (Seoul: Bank of Korea, 1966), pp. 10–11.

13. Haptong News Agency, *Korea Annual 1967* (Seoul: Haptong News Agency, 1967), p. 137.

14. For a complete breakdown of voting records by election district and province, see *Tonga Ilbo*, May 5, 1967.

15. For a complete list of candidates for each district as well as party nominees for proportional representation seats, see *ibid.*, May 16, 1967.

16. *Ibid.*, June 6, 1967.

17. Republic of Korea, Central Election Management Commission, *Yŏkde kukhoe ŭiwŏn sŏnkŏ sanghang* (The Patterns of Successive National Assembly Elections) (Seoul: Chungang sŏnkŏ kwanri wiwŏnhoe, 1967), p. 723.

18. *New York Times*, June 9, 1967.

19. Park's statement was made on May 26 in Mokpo, where one of the bitterest contests took place between the ruling party and the opposition candidates (*Tonga Ilbo*, May 26, 1967).

20. Republic of Korea, Supreme Council for National Reconstruction, *A Commentary on the Constitution of the Republic of Korea As Submitted to National Referendum* (Seoul: n. pub., 1962), p. 10.

21. *New York Times*, June 16, 1967.

22. *Japan Times*, June 22, 1967.

23. *Tonga Ilbo*, July 11, 1967.

24. "Pujŏng sŏnkŏrŭl ttajinda" (Contesting the Rigged Elections), *Shindonga*, July, 1967, pp. 96–107, and related articles on the same theme, pp. 72–132.

25. July 13, 1967.

26. June 20, 1967.

27. For the full text of Park's inaugural address, see *Tonga Ilbo*, July 1, 1967.

28. *New York Times*, July 4, 1967.

Conclusion

1. Edward W. Wagner, "Failure in Korea," *Foreign Affairs*, XXXX, no. 1 (Oct., 1961), 129.

Bibliography

This bibliography is not meant to be general and exhaustive, and includes only those publications which the author has actually used in writing this study. The author consulted and benefited from many other worthy publications.

Books

Allen, Richard C. *Korea's Syngman Rhee*. Rutland, Vt.: Tuttle, 1960.

Almond, Gabriel A., and James S. Coleman, eds. *The Politics of the Developing Areas*. Princeton: Princeton University Press, 1960.

Bank of Korea. *Economic Statistical Yearbook 1966*. Seoul: Bank of Korea, 1966.

Cho, Pyŏng-ok (Chough Pyong-ok). *Minjujuŭiwa na* (Democracy and I). Seoul: Yŏngsin munhwasa, 1959.

——. *Naŭi hoegorok* (My Recollections). Seoul: Mingyosa, 1959.

Cho, T'ak-sŏng, ed. *Sawŏl hyŏngmyŏng* (April Revolution). Seoul: Ch'angwŏnsa, 1960.

Ch'oe, Ŭng-sang. *Nongjŏng simnyŏnsa* (The Ten-Year History of the Administration of Agriculture). Seoul: Semunsa, 1959.

Chŏng, Il-hyŏng. *U.N. kwa hanguk munjae* (The U.N. and the Korean Problem). Seoul: Korean Association for the United Nations, 1961.

Ch'ŏngyang yukbŏp p'yŏnch'an wiwŏnhoe. *Yukbŏp chŏnsŏ* (Complete Six Codes). Seoul: Ch'ŏngyang Codification Committee of the Six Codes, 1961.

Conlon Associates, Ltd. *United States Foreign Policy: Asia.* Washington, D.C.: Government Printing Office, 1957.

Goodrich, Leland M. *Korea: A Study of U.S. Policy in the United Nations.* New York: Council of Foreign Relations, 1956.

Gordenker, Leon. *The United Nations and the Peaceful Unification of Korea.* The Hague: Martinus Nijhoff, 1959.

Hakwŏnsa. *Korea: Its Land, People and Culture of All Ages.* Seoul: Hakwŏnsa, 1960.

Han, T'ae-su. *Hanguk chŏngdangsa* (A History of Korean Political Parties). Seoul: Sin t'aeyangsa, 1961.

Hanguk hyŏngmyŏng chaep'ansa p'yŏnchan wiwŏnhoe. *Hanguk hyŏngmyŏng chaep'ansa* (The History of Revolutionary Trials in Korea). Seoul: Hanguk hyŏngmyŏng chaep'ansa p'yŏnchan wiwŏnhoe, 1962.

Hanguk kunsa hyŏngmyŏngsa p'yŏnchan wiwŏnhoe. *Hanguk kunsa hyŏngmyŏngsa* (The History of the Korean Military Revolution). Vols. I-A, I-B, III. Seoul: Tonga sŏjŏk hoesa, 1963.

Haptong News Agency. *Korea Annual 1964.* Seoul: Haptong News Agency, 1964.

———. *Korea Annual 1967.* Seoul: Haptong News Agency, 1967.

Kang, Chin-hwa, ed. *Taehan minguk kŏnguk simnyŏnji* (The Ten-Year History of the Nation-Building of the Republic of Korea). Seoul: Kŏnguk simnyŏnji kanhenghoe, 1956.

Kunsa hyŏngmyŏngsa p'yŏnchan wiwŏnhoe. *Oilyuk kunsa hyŏngmyŏngŭi chŏnmo* (The Entire Picture of the Military Revolution of May 16). Seoul: Munkwansa, 1964.

Lee, Chong-sik. *The Politics of Korean Nationalism.* Berkeley: University of California Press, 1963.

McCune, George M. *Korea Today.* London: Allen and Unwin, 1950.

———. *Korea's Postwar Political Problems.* New York: Institute of Pacific Relations, 1947.

Meade, E. Grant. *American Military Government in Korea.* New York: King's Crown Press, 1951.

Millis, Walter S., ed. *The Forrestal Diaries.* New York: Viking, 1951.

Min, Yong-bin, ed. *Sawŏlŭi yŏngungdŭl* (April Heroes). Seoul: Ilsinsa, 1960.

Oliver, Robert T. *Syngman Rhee: The Man behind the Myth.* New York: Dodd, Mead, 1954.

Ŏm, Sang-sŏp. *Kwŏllyŏkkwa chayu* (Authority and Freedom). Seoul: Kyŏngku ch'ulp'ansa, 1957.

Paek, Nam-ju, ed. *Hyŏngmyŏng chidoja Pak Chŏng-hi non* (On Chung Hee Park, the Revolutionary Leader). Seoul: Inmulkaesa, 1961.

Park, Chung Hee. *Chidojado* (The Ways of a Leader). Seoul: Kukka chaekŏn ch'oego hoeŭi, 1961.

——. *Kukkawa hyŏngmyŏngkwa na* (The Country, the Revolution and I). Trans. Leon Sinder. Seoul: Hyangmunsa, 1963.

——. *Uri minjokŭi nagalkil* (The Path for Our Nation). Seoul: Tonga ch'ulpansa, 1962.

Reeve, W. D. *The Republic of Korea: A Political and Economic Study.* London: Oxford University Press, 1963.

Rosinger, Lawrence K. *The State of Asia.* New York: Knopf, 1951.

Rossiter, Clinton L. *Constitutional Dictatorship: Crisis Government in Modern Democracies.* Princeton: Princeton University Press, 1948.

Sawŏl hyŏngmyŏng ch'ŏngsa p'yŏnch'anhoe. *Sawŏl hyŏngmyŏng ch'ŏngsa* (The Annals of the April Revolution). Seoul: Sŏnggongsa, 1960.

Scalapino, Robert A., ed. *North Korea Today.* New York: Praeger, 1963.

So, Pyŏng-jo. *Chukwŏnjaŭi chŭngŏn: Hanguk taeŭi chŏngch'isa* (Testimonies of the Sovereign: A History of Representative Government in Korea). Seoul: Moŭm ch'ulp'ansa, 1963.

Tewskbury, Donald G., ed. *Source Materials on Korean Politics and Ideologies.* New York: Institute of Pacific Relations, 1950.

Truman, Harry S. *Memoirs.* 2 vols.; Vol. II. Garden City: Doubleday, 1956.

Yi, Ki-ha. *Hanguk chŏngdang paltalsa* (A History of the Development of Korean Political Parties). Seoul: Ŭihoe chŏngch'isa, 1961.

Yu, cha-hu. *Chŏsŏn minju sasangsa* (A History of Democratic Ideas in Korea). Seoul: Chŏsŏn kumyung chohap yŏnhaphoe, 1949.

Articles

Allen, Richard C. "South Korea: The New Regime," *Pacific Affairs*, XXXIV, no. 1 (Spring, 1961), 54–57.
Barr, John M. "The Second Republic of Korea," *Far Eastern Survey*, XXIX, no. 9 (Sept., 1960), 129–132.
"Biographical Sketch of General Chung Hee Park," *Korean Observer*, Aug., 1963.
Bradner, Stephen. "Korea: Experiment and Instability," *Japan Quarterly*, VIII, no. 4 (Oct.–Dec., 1961), 412–420.
Briggs, Walter. "The Military Revolution in Korea: On Its Leader and Achievements," *Koreana Quarterly*, V, no. 2 (Summer, 1963), 17–34.
Cho, Il-mun. "Chŏngch'i p'adongŭi insikkwa pip'an" (An Understanding and Criticism of the Political Crisis), *Shinch'ŏnji*, III, no. 1 (April, 1953), 31–43.
Cho, Ka-gyŏng. "Hyŏngmyŏng chuch'aeŭi chŏngsinjŏk honmi" (Spiritual Confusion of the Main Body of the Revolution), *Sasangge Monthly*, IX, no. 4 (April, 1961), 70–79.
Chŏng, Chae-ho. "Pak Chŏng-hi," *Saedae*, III, no. 3 (April, 1965), 138.
Chu, Sŏk-kyun. "T'am-o ron" (Essay on Corrupt Officials), *Sasangge Monthly*, I, no. 5 (Aug., 1953), 178.
Chung, Young-iob. "Economic Development and Population Growth in South Korea during 1953–1971" (unpublished paper presented to the 16th annual meeting of the Midwest Conference on Asian Affairs, Nov., 1967).
Dull, Paul S. "South Korean Constitution," *Far Eastern Survey*, XVII, no. 17 (Sept. 8, 1948), 205–207.
Earl, David M. "Korea: The Meaning of the Second Republic," *Far Eastern Survey*, XXIX, no. 11 (Nov., 1960), 169–175.
Gordenker, Leon. "The United Nations, the United States Occupation and the 1948 Election in Korea," *Political Science Quarterly*, LXXIII, no. 3 (Sept., 1948), 426–450.

Hahn, Bae-ho, and Kim Kyu-taik. "Korean Political Leaders (1952–1962): Their Social Origins and Skills," *Asian Survey*, III, no. 7 (July, 1963).

Han, T'ae-yŏn. "Chei konghwaguk hŏnbŏpŭi kyŏnghyang" (The Tendency of the Constitution of the Second Republic), *Sasangge Monthly*, VIII, no. 6 (June, 1960), 165–173.

——. "Hanguk yadangŭi sahoehak" (Sociology of the Korean Opposition Parties), *Sasangge Monthly*, VIII, no. 2 (Feb., 1960), 20–28.

Han, Tai-soo. "Results of National Referendum and Its Significance," *Koreana Quarterly*, V, no. 1 (April, 1963), 7.

Hong, I-sŏp. "Sawŏl hyŏngmyŏngŭi chaep'yŏngka" (Reappraisal of the April Revolution), *Sasangge Monthly*, IX, no. 4 (April, 1961), 54–59.

Hong, Sung-chick. "A Pilot Study of the Korean Students' Values," *Korean Affairs*, II, no. 1 (1963), 1–11.

Kang, In-sŏp. "Minjudang chŏngkwŏn ch'oehuŭi nal" (The Last Day of the Democratic Regime), *Shindonga*, May, 1965.

——. "Sawŏl hyŏngmyŏng hugi" (A Postscript to the April Revolution), *Shindonga*, April, 1965.

——. "Yuksa p'algi seng" (The Eighth Graduating Class of the Military Academy), *Shindonga*, Sept., 1964.

Kim, C. I. Eugene, and Kim Ke-soo. "The April 1960 Student Movement," *A Pattern of Political Development: Korea*, ed. C. I. Eugene Kim (Kalamazoo, Mich.: Korea Research and Publications, 1964).

Kim, Ki-bŏm. "Certain Features of the Constitution," *Korean Affairs*, III, no. 1 (April, 1964), 20.

Kim, Myon-whai. "The Presidential Election in Korea, 1963," *Korean Affairs*, II, nos. 3–4 (Oct., 1963), 372.

Kim, Nam-jin. "Sahoe kujowa hŏnbŏp chilsŏ" (Social Structure and Constitutional Order), *Sasangge Monthly*, IX, no. 7 (July, 1961), 48–60.

Kim, Sŏng-t'ae. "Sawŏl sipkuilŭi simnihak" (Psychology of April 19), *Sasangge Monthly*, IX, no. 4 (April, 1961), 78–85.

Kim, Yong-sang. "Hŏnbŏpŭl ssagodonŭn kukhoe p'ungkyŏng" (The National Assembly Scene on the Problem of the Constitution), *Shinch'ŏnji*, III, no. 6 (July, 1948), 25–26.

——. "Kukhoeŭi tongt'ewa kŭmhuŭi munje" (The Complexion

of the National Assembly and the Problems of the Future), *Shinch'ŏnji*, III, no. 4 (June, 1948), 21–30.

Kim, Yong-sŏn. "Kukhoe sŏngŏ" (National Assembly Elections), *Sasangge Monthly*, IV, no. 8 (Aug., 1956), 57–62.

Kim, Yŏng-su. " 'Minju konghwadang' sajŏn chojik" (The Advance Organization of the "Democratic Republican Party"), *Shindonga*, Nov., 1964, 168–173.

Korea Informer, July–Aug., 1962.

Lee, Joung-sik. "The Social Origin of Members of the Sixth National Assembly," *Korean Affairs*, III, no. 1 (April, 1964), 15.

Levi, Werner. "Fate of Democracy in South and Southeast Asia," *Far Eastern Quarterly*, XXVIII (Feb., 1959), 25–29.

McCune, George M. "The Korean Situation," *Far Eastern Survey*, XVII, no. 17 (Sept. 8, 1948), 197–202.

"Military Purification Movement Leads to 1961 May Revolution," *Korean Report*, II, no. 4 (May, 1962), 10.

Min, Sŏk-hong. "Hyŏndaesawa chayu minjujuŭi: Sawŏl hyŏng-myŏngŭi ihaelŭl wihayŏ" (Contemporary History and Liberal Democracy: For an Understanding of the April Revolution), *Sasangge Monthly*, VIII, no. 6 (June, 1960), 90–98.

Oh, John Kie-chiang. "Post-coup Korea on a Treadmill: A Political Analysis," *East-West Center Review*, II, no. 2 (Oct., 1965), 1–15.

Park, Chung Hee. "Korean Political Philosophy: Administrative Democracy," *Korean Affairs*, II (May–June, 1962), 111–121.

"Pujŏng sŏnkŏrŭl ttajinda" (Contesting the Rigged Elections), *Shindonga*, July, 1967, pp. 95–107.

Scalapino, Robert A. "Korea: The Politics of Change," *Asian Survey*, III, no. 1 (Jan., 1963).

Sin, Sang-ch'o. "Yi Sŭng-man p'okchŏngŭi chongyŏn" (The End of the Tyranny of Syngman Rhee), *Sasangge Monthly*, VIII, no. 6 (June, 1960), 82–89.

Sin, Sŏk-ho. "Chayudang sŏngnip ijŏnŭi chŏngjŏng" (The Political Situation before the Formation of the Liberal Party), in *Hanguk hyŏngmyŏng chaep'ansa p'yŏnch'an wiwŏnhoe*, *Hankuk hyŏngmyŏng chaep'ansa* (The History of Revolutionary Trials in Korea) (Seoul: Hanguk hyŏngmyŏng chaep'ansa p'yŏnch'an wiwŏnhoe, 1962), Vol. I.

Sunoo, Harold W. "Possibility of 'Koreanic' Democracy," *Korea Journal*, I, no. 1 (Sept., 1961), 4–5.

Wagner, Edward W. "Failure in Korea," *Foreign Affairs*, XL, no. 1 (Oct., 1961), 128–135.

Weems, C. N. "Korea: Dilemma of an Underdeveloped Country," *Foreign Policy Association Headline Series*, no. 144 (Nov.–Dec., 1960).

Yi, Chŏng-sik. "Cheyukde taet'ongnyŏng sŏnkŏŭi ŭii" (The Significance of the Sixth Presidential Elections), *Shindonga*, June, 1967, pp. 68–83.

Yi, Kŭk-ch'an. "Chŏngch'ijŏk mugwansimkwa minjujuŭi wigi" (Political Apathy and the Crisis of Democracy), *Sasangge Monthly*, IX, no. 4 (April, 1961), 60–69.

Yim, Hong-bin. "An Analysis of the General Election in 1963," *Korean Affairs*, III, no. 1 (April, 1964), 125.

Yu, Hyŏk-in. "Pak taet'ongnyŏngŭl umjiginŭn saramdŭl" (Those Who Move President Park), *Shindonga*, Oct., 1964.

Yun, Ch'ŏn-ju. "Pujŏng sŏngŏŭi pangjŏngsik" (Formulae for Rigged Elections), *Sasangge Monthly*, VIII, no. 7 (June, 1960), 109–118.

Official Publications and Documents

Korean Research and Information Office. *Korea Report: Reports from the Cabinet Ministers of the Republic of Korea*. Washington, D.C.: 1959. VI, 104–106.

Republic of Korea. *Kwanpo* (Official Gazette), no. 2206, Dec. 26, 1958.

Republic of Korea, Central Election Management Commission. *Yŏkde kukhoe ŭiwŏn sŏnkŏ sanghang* (The Patterns of Successive National Assembly Elections). Seoul: Chungang sŏnkŏ kwanri wiwŏnhoe, 1967.

Republic of Korea, Ministry of Foreign Affairs. *The Military Revolution in Korea*. Seoul: Taehan minguk oemubu, 1961.

Republic of Korea, National Assembly. *Ch'amgo charyo* (Reference Materials). Vol. XVI. Seoul: Minŭiwŏn samuch'ŏ, 1959.

——. *Kukhoe simnyŏnji* (The Ten-Year Record of the National Assembly). Seoul: Minŭiwŏn samuch'ŏ, 1958.

——. *Taehan minguk kukhoe kaekwan* (Survey of the National Assembly of the Republic of Korea). Seoul: Minŭiwŏn samuch'ŏ, 1959.

Republic of Korea, Supreme Council for National Reconstruction. *A Commentary on the Constitution of the Republic of Korea As Submitted to National Referendum.* Seoul: no publisher, 1962.

——. *Military Revolution in Korea.* Seoul: The Secretariat of the Supreme Council for National Reconstruction, 1961.

U.N. Doc. A/AC/19/80; Doc. A/AC/19/80, Add. 1; Doc. A/AC/19/66, Add. 3; Doc. A/575, Add. 2; Doc. A/583; Doc. A/4900.

——. Press Release 70, June 30, 1948.

U.N., General Assembly. *Official Records,* 18th sess., supp. no. 12A–A5512, Add. 1.

——. Resolution 195 (III), Dec. 12, 1948.

U.S., Agency for International Development. *U.S. Foreign Assistance and Assistance from International Organizations.* Washington, D.C.: Government Printing Office, 1962.

U.S., Congress, Senate, Committee on Foreign Relations. *The United States and the Korean Problem: Documents 1943–1953.* 83rd Cong., 1st sess. Washington, D.C.: Government Printing Office, 1953.

U.S., Department of State. *A Historical Summary of United States–Korean Relations: With a Chronology of Important Developments, 1834–1962.* Washington, D.C.: Government Printing Office, 1962.

——. *Korea 1945 to 1948.* Washington, D.C.: Government Printing Office, 1948.

——. *The Record on Korean Unification, 1943–1960: Narrative Summary with Principal Documents.* Washington, D.C.: Government Printing Office, 1960.

——, Historical Office. *American Foreign Policy: Current Documents 1960.* Washington, D.C.: Government Printing Office, 1964.

——, Historical Office. *American Foreign Policy: Current Docu-*

ments 1961. Washington, D.C.: Government Printing Office, 1965.

——, Office of Public Affairs. *Problems of Greece, Korea, and Palestine.* Washington, D.C.: Government Printing Office, 1949.

Index